Do It Yourself

Psychic Power

Do It Yourself
Psychic Power

Natalia O'Sullivan

Practical Tools and Techniques
for Awakening Your Natural Gifts

*To all those who through the years have offered
invaluable advice and help from the Spirit World.
&
To my wonderful husband Terry for all his support
and to my children Sequoia, Ossian and Bede for
their patience and generosity of spirit.*

Element
An Imprint of HarperCollins*Publishers*
77-85 Fulham Palace Road
Hammersmith, London w6 8JB

ELEMENT

and *Element*
are trademarks of HarperCollins*Publishers* Ltd
Published by Element 2002

10 9 8 7 6 5 4 3 2 1

Copyright © Natalia O'Sullivan 2002

Natalia O'Sullivan asserts the moral right
to be identified as the author of this work

A catalogue record for this book is
available from the British Library

ISBN 0-00-712998-x

Printed and bound in Great Britain by
Scotprint, Haddington, East Lothian

Contents

Foreword

My intention in writing this book is to help people develop their natural psychic powers so that they can become a part of their daily life. Psychic ability is a gift that allows us to take on life's challenges, to be one step ahead, to learn how to read and recognize the subtle messages in life, or to learn to receive messages from our soul or from our spirit guides. We learn how to do this by becoming aware not just of a physical reality, but also of the subtle reality of the spiritual world which encompasses it. This requires a great leap of understanding for many people since we have grown up in an age that neglects or ignores subtle reality – despite the fact that millions of people read their daily horoscope, visit psychics and fortune tellers and go on the Internet for a quick-fix tarot reading.

You may think it implausible that you are psychic, yet I expect you have often sensed that something is going to happen or that someone is about to call – and it does or they do! We may pass these off as hunches but in truth they are the result of different types of psychic powers: sensing the future is precognition and knowing who is about to call is a form of telepathy. Many talented psychics have denied or suppressed their powers only to find that once they have taken that shot in the dark, experienced that moment of discovery, life makes sense and a whole new spectrum of living opens up.

How to Use this Book

This book is not intended to blast open otherworldly gates so that you are sucked inside. It is designed to help you find the doors and pathways already in your life. It will help you discover

what resonates within you so that you are able to call back from your soul and ancestral heritage the psychic gifts that you already possess.

To this end, I have concentrated on practical advice and exercises. This will help you develop your psychic skills and incorporate them into your everyday life. To help you identify with the concept of psychic powers proposed in this book, I have also included some of the experiences of people I know and admire.

It is not my intention to alienate any reader from her or his spiritual tradition; the practice of psychic power is compatible with the practice of any spirituality. It may even provoke a more profound appreciation of your religion's mystical application or bring to you a wider understanding of how to work with your spiritual life in a mystical way.

Please read these guidelines before you read the main text.

- Read this book through at least once and understand the concepts and principles before attempting any of the practical exercises.
- I have tried to keep the text and information as up-to-date as possible so some of the information may challenge the more ancient traditions of psychic development and spiritualism.
- This book will not qualify you as a psychic practitioner, but if you wish to use your psychic powers to help others then seek out a personal teacher (see Resources on page 180). Ensure that you know how to work with your gift and have an understanding of protection before you teach, help or counsel others.
- Try the exercises the way they are set out here. If they don't work for you after a series of good and sequential attempts, then adapt them intelligently and creatively, using your own spiritual guidelines and techniques.
- Do not mix these practices with others you have learned in other non-psychic disciplines and do not treat any exercise as a psychological or therapeutic technique.
- Keep a journal or diary to monitor your development as this will enable you to see how much your psychic powers grow over a period of practice.
- Keep your sense of proportion by regularly, preferably daily, visiting the natural world, exercising your body and keeping yourself healthy.
- Keep your sense of self-importance in check with humour and common sense.
- Finally, enjoy the unfolding of your psychic powers.

Introduction to psychic powers

Psychic powers are natural and intuitive – everyone can develop their psychic potential if they wish to. Developing this skill is not only a means of connecting with the spirit world; it helps us achieve greater awareness and control over our destiny.

Psychic awareness is the natural ability to perceive things before they happen – even guessing lottery numbers and winning on a horse race may have its basis in one's psychic ability. We are all psychics to varying degrees of sensitivity. If we observe nature it's obvious that animals sense a presence long before it can be seen; this is essential for their survival. We use this same intuitive source – in our work, during competitive sports or business situations – to survive in the modern world. Our gut instinct helps us to connect with a sixth sense, or second sight, which in turn helps us to 'tune in' to places and people – both past and future.

There is no need to follow a spiritual path or to have strict religious tendencies to be an accurate psychic, but in most traditions training is required in order to develop accurate psychic skills. Each psychic works on many different energy frequencies and, if we have the necessary skill, these can dictate to us our future profession. Being psychic can be a bonus to the lucky ones and a curse to others.

What qualities make a good psychic?

- *Personality:* Psychics tend to be bright, naturally intelligent and extrovert. People with more out-going personalities score more in psychic tests than those who are sombre, shy and reflective.

- *Sensitivity:* Do you find that you get easily hurt and are oversensitive to people and atmospheres? Most psychics are also extremely sensitive individuals and even in child-hood would have been considered oversensitive.
- *Creativity:* Are you artistic? A large proportion of psychics come from an artistic or creative background. Some psychic researchers suggest that this is because psychics, like artists, predominantly use the right-hand side of the brain – the side that is creative and intuitive.
- *Dreams:* Do you have vivid and colourful dreams? Dreaming is one of the routes to the subconscious mind. If you are in tune with your inner self, then you naturally become aware of your psychic self during sleep.
- *Perception and sight:* Do you see bright lights around living things? If so, this is the ability to 'see' the aura, the magnetic field around living things. The aura is known to change shape and colour depending on the mood or energy levels of a person or living thing. If you can see this – and even the colour of the aura – then you are very psychic.
- *Intuition:* Do you listen to your intuition? Do you have a gut instinct or can you sense things about people, situations or places. Much of the information that we receive through intuition is gained through sensitivity and connecting through the solar plexus into another person or situation. Intuition is listening to your inner self and hearing advice from the spirit world.

Are You Psychic?

Think not? Well, you may be more psychic than you think. If you trust your natural instincts about things you will begin to realize that these instincts are as natural and normal as any of our five physical senses – the abilities to see, hear, touch, taste and smell.

Our own unique psychic potential utilizes our ability to be able to receive, access and transmit vast quantities of information from our day-to-day life. This takes place within an aspect of our mind that tunes into a psychic or unseen frequency. We can learn to strengthen, access and make use of these abilities, whether it is for the simplest of tasks or a life-threatening situation – for instance, choosing a job or profession, trusting your judgment about a partner or deciding when to have children. The act of being able to see beyond most situations means you can avoid being in the wrong place at the wrong time and avoid making wrong decisions. Psychic awareness is there to help guide and inform you of future problems and opportunities.

Are You Naturally Psychic?

Have you experienced any of the following?

- Do you frequently phone your mother or friend only to find their number engaged as they are trying to phone you? Or do they say that they were thinking about you when you called?
- Have you ever decided on impulse to change your route to work, only to discover later that there was an accident or an unusual traffic problem on your customary route?
- You meet someone new who appears to be 'perfect' but something inside tells you that you should distrust them – then later you discover your reservations were justified.
- You phone a friend on impulse, feeling that there is something wrong and they confirm that there had been a disaster at work, in their love life or a family crisis.
- Sometimes your dreams are so vivid that you feel they are real, then the next day you find that your dream comes true.
- You suddenly think of someone you have not seen or heard from in years and the next day you receive a letter, e-mail or call from them.
- You waken seconds before your baby, despite the fact they are in another room and have no regular sleeping patterns.
- You book into a hotel and find that there is a bad atmosphere, you cannot sleep and you sense that it could be haunted. When you check it out with the hotel they confirm that the place has been known to be haunted.
- You have a mother or grandmother who is psychic (psychic abilities run in the family).
- You have seen lights around people's heads – perhaps since you were a child and were surprised that other people did not.
- You have heard voices of dead people or sense someone standing behind you when there is no one there.
- You can make things happen with thought or intent.
- You have always been very sympathetic to other people and feel other's pain and suffering.
- You possess the ability to make people feel better and can detect a warmth coming from your hands when extending affection or wanting to soothe another's pain.
- You sense dangerous moments before they happen or have disaster dreams that come true.

If you recognize four or more of these experiences then your psychic powers are already well tuned. Even if you only relate to one or two of these statements, your psychic abilities are still present. Maybe your natural psychic abilities were present in your childhood but were not encouraged, so you relied on your five physical senses and logic alone.

Being able to connect to your psychic potential enables you to use your intuitive and psychic senses as if they were as natural and normal as using your mind to create ideas and make decisions. To see beyond the reality that you are living gives you the opportunity to be one step ahead. This can allow you to feel comfortable in your own skin – often for the first time. Many people who have been psychic since childhood have been unable to acknowledge the feelings or sensations they experienced as a child or teenager for fear of alarming others.

Being a Psychic

Some of us are using our psychic gifts without even realizing we are doing it. We are aware of the information that we receive through an 'inner' sense but do not talk about it – often fearing that other people will not understand.

There is a common misunderstanding that psychic power is something that some people possess and others do not. The reality is more complicated: we all have the ability to be psychic, but some people are just more awake to their powers than others. Everyone has the potential and each individual's potential is unique.

Awakening these gifts and utilizing them to support your personal and spiritual life is a journey that takes time, support from good teachers and mentors, and discipline. It is your choice whether or not you develop your latent psychic gifts. This is similar to learning how to play an instrument: you must have both the passion and the *patience* to learn before you can become a talented player.

Opening Up to Your Psychic Gift

Some people are fascinated by human psychological and emotional characteristics, and often their psychic gift will be an ability to tune into a person's personality and see their weaknesses and strengths. Other people have the gift of vision – of seeing into the past and future of individuals, a place or a situation. We could call them fortune tellers or diviners. They will have a natural vision which will come to them in dreams whilst they are asleep, through daydreaming thoughts and inspirations, or from just having a knowing feeling that something good or bad may happen. Other people see visions: for instance, a place or circumstance causes a *deja vu* experience that brings forward an inner sight of a situation or circumstance which may have happened or is going to happen.

One of the most accessible methods of psychic development is psychometry – the ability to see psychically by using touch. Many people find it a good first step in encouraging their psychic gifts to open up. In the majority of cases strong psychic abilities tend to be hereditary. They do, however, commonly skip a generation so parents are often uninterested in spiritual or psychic matters and find it strange that a child of theirs should be drawn to study these traditions. Such children learn to be quiet about their 'strange' feelings and it is often only when they begin to uncover their gifts that they also discover that a grandparent or great-grandparent was psychic.

Psychic abilities can be separated into nine main categories:

TELEPATHY is the ability to tune in to the thoughts of others and to be able to project your own thoughts into another person's mind.

PRECOGNITION is a knowledge of events before they take place – enabling you to make predictions about the future.

DIVINATION is the ability to see into the future by using psychic tools such as crystal balls, tarot cards and tea leaves.

PSYCHOMETRY is seeing without eyes – the ability to 'tune' into objects to be able to read a person's character and even tell their past or future.

DREAMING is the ability to tune into psychic frequencies while sleeping and bring the information back into everyday life by interpreting the symbols and images seen in dreams.

SPIRIT COMMUNICATION is the ability to communicate with spirits either by being overshadowed by a spirit's presence or through direct communication. It is also called channelling or mediumship.

CLAIRSENTIENCE is to be able to smell and sense what is unseen.

CLAIRVOYANCE is being able to see mentally what is happening in a dimension that is unseen or out of sight. It is a term that means exceptional sight.

CLAIRAUDIENCE is the faculty to hear what is beyond the normal range of hearing.

I hear so many stories from people who have had psychic encounters without recognizing them. For example, knowing if a family member or close friend is in trouble without speaking to them first, or averting disaster by listening to their intuition about road traffic. These are simple intuitive responses to your day-to-day life but when you take these innate skills a step further, you will enhance your ability to see through people, hear and feel spirits, see auras and colours in the atmosphere and divine the future.

Connecting With Our Psychic Energy

Mankind is an ancient being and evolution's long memory is locked away within each of us. Our DNA has encoded within it ancient patterns of behaviour that once helped us survive in a harsh environment. In today's modern world, most of our inherited behaviour patterns are obsolete and no longer necessary for survival. Yet they still lie dormant in the unconscious, ready to re-animate should they be needed again.

Below the thin layer of brain called the cerebral cortex, where the rational mind functions, lies the 90 per cent of our being that we are unaware of – the primitive, reptilian brain. Within this aspect of the mind lies our subconscious connection with our ancestors and their ancient knowledge. When we are able to access this memory or connection, we are able to draw from the powers within our subconscious mind and this is where that aspect of our spirit talks to us about who we are and what we want from our lives.

Let's look in more detail at the varying kinds of psychic ability.

Telepathy

Telepathy is an exchange of information directly from the mind of one individual to the mind of another without the need for words to be spoken aloud or any exchange of physical, non-verbal communication such as eye signals, hand gestures or other forms of body language.

We are all telepathic to some degree and go about our daily lives transmitting and receiving information – often without being consciously aware that we are doing so. While we each transmit and receive in different ways, the basic principle is the same: we all act like radios, tuning into information and sending out signals on certain frequencies. Some of us have a greater ability to receive; others are more able to transmit. Some people are on the same frequency and therefore find it easier to receive telepathic messages than others. Many people discover that as they become closer in a physical relationship they begin to connect with that person on a telepathic level. Mothers and daughters have a natural link, particularly as the psychic gift is passed down the mother line from both parents into their descendants.

Our individual telepathic abilities are closely linked to our other psychic gifts. If we are more clairvoyant than clairaudient, for example, then we are much more likely to receive our telepathic information in the form of visual images or symbols than to 'hear' the thoughts of other people in our head. A telepathic clairsentient may receive a sense of another person's physical or emotional state, even at a distance.

Telepathy can operate at short distances or at great ones. We experience short distance telepathy with family members and friends. In these cases, our telepathic abilities become entwined with our other abilities to read and transmit information and to tune into our intuition. For instance, we often know when someone we know well is angry with us, even when they do not express it openly. We may pick up a combination of signals that includes body language, tone of voice, changes in behaviour and clairsentient emotional messages, as well as telepathic thoughts that the person transmits – and we receive loud and clear.

Long distance telepathy can be just as common, though it can appear more remarkable because we do not have the more obvious physical signals to rely on. On many occasions I have thought of a friend abroad and then received a letter or e-mail from them.

Developing Telepathic Communication

Good telepathic communication, when combined with good physical and verbal communication skills, can be very useful for creating harmonious relationships at home and at work. Very few people are so telepathic that they can read another person's mind as easily as reading a book. To develop accurate telepathic skills takes practice and patience. Begin by trying it out with a friend or a member of your family.

Sit opposite each other and take it in turns. Hold a thought in your mind, just a simple word, and then create an image in your head that symbolizes the word. For instance, think heart – see a red-coloured heart in your mind's eye. Hold the image for five minutes and project that image to the person opposite you. After five minutes ask them what they saw in your mind. Practise this with the same person over a few days and you will become more confident in your ability to send and receive telepathic messages.

Developing good telepathic skills assists with spirit communication, clairvoyance and clairaudience skills, as accurate transmission of information can only happen when you have clear vision and are able to telepathically tune into people, spirits and places.

Precognition

This is the ability to see into the future through dreams and daytime impressions. Have you ever dreamed of a future event and it has happened? Have you ever visited a place and felt that you had been there before? Have you ever been at a social event and knew how the evening would turn out? Have you seen into the future and and been able to foretell which of your childhood friends would do well and which would fail? This is precognition.

Nostradamus (1503–66) was the greatest seer in the Western world. To open his vision he would focus his attention on a bowl of water. He would then see pictures projected from his mind and relate these to his knowledge of astrology. In this manner he predicted many major European historical events including the Great Fire of London, Hitler's rise to power and the nuclear bomb.

To develop this skill you don't necessarily need to use a bowl of water, a crystal ball or any type of paraphernalia (although these can make things easier for beginners). To practise precognition you need to be able to open your mind and have a focal point on which to fix your attention. I have found that the most sensitive time of day for this type of psychic connection is late at night, when you are tired and unable to focus your concentration on everyday reality. The more tired I am, the more open I become to receive psychic information and to be able to see into the future.

The best form of development exercise for precognition is to work on divination skills using tools such as tarot cards, scrying through crystals balls or a bowl of water, or even reading tea leaves – any form of concentration that opens up your natural ability to see into the future.

Divination

All techniques for predicting the future are based on interpreting random events – whether it is the fall of coins or runes, the patterns in sand or smoke stains on a mirror. That random event then takes on a special meaning when we ask it to be our oracle.

The use of tarot cards is a common form of divination. I have studied them since my teens, using them as a tool with which to tune into my clairvoyant skills. I have used these skills to help people work out their personal problems and to help see me through certain challenges and crossroads in my life. The cards are generally beautifully illustrated and it is with the imagery of the illustrations that the magic or power of the tarot lies. Learning about these symbols can take years of practice and reading but once learnt they are never forgotten.

Tarot Cards

GETTING STARTED

At first glance, traditional tarot cards appear difficult to understand. The cards were originally designed when most of the world's population was illiterate, and much of the knowledge was passed down by Romany oral traditions. The pictures and the symbols told a story and gave inspiration to the diviner, so in essence the cards are simple to read as they work by triggering your own intuition rather than being based on a technical understanding of the symbology within the cards.

Many cards and their accompanying books are overloaded with so much information – including astrology, psychology, world religious symbols, numerology and so on – that I found it was best to choose a set of cards whose colour, texture and tradition I responded to. (I began my journey with the Rider tarot designed by A.E. Waite, a pack based on the European tradition, but now I work with Dakini Oracle cards based on Tibetan Buddhism – choose whatever suits you.)

If you are going to work with the cards on other people, they must be bought for you as a gift. So even if you have chosen them, ask your partner or a friend to buy them for you. Buy the accompanying book with the cards so at least you can study the meanings and format of laying the cards out. Keep your tarot cards in a soft, natural-fibred cloth, preferably red in colour, as this protects them and holds their power.

Before you start practising, get to know the cards. Look at each one and decide what it is trying to tell you. How would you interpret the card in a reading? What does it say about the emotional, spiritual or material conditions of a person? Devote a good deal of time to this before you look up the standard meanings of the cards from the book, as it will help you link your own intuitive response to the cards. When you have decided on your interpretation, compare it with the meanings in your book and you will probably find that your interpretation comes close to the established meaning. Practise on yourself and on close friends and family until you feel comfortable working with them without referring to the book.

THE CARDS

In the traditional tarot there are 78 cards, divided into two main groups: 22 Major Arcana, numbered 0-21; and 56 Minor Arcana, divided into four suits. The Major Arcana is the most powerful of the set, symbolizing the journey of the man in the pack, called 'the fool', in his encounters with the characters within the Major Arcana set. Some people prefer using only the Major Arcana cards and get to know these first before introducing the rest of the pack. The Minor Arcana is divided into four suits as in a playing card set – Wands, Cups, Swords and Coins.

The cards can be shuffled so that they are upright or reversed (when the cards' meaning then changes). The cards contain an equal balance of positive and negative so reversing the cards adds little to the overall reading and most of the time I ignore the reverse and work with the meaning only in the upright position. You can do many different types of readings, from simple questions and answers to more elaborate combinations.

It is said that it is impossible to read the tarot for yourself, and unfortunately in some cases this is true as wishful thinking and inner fears and expectations can get in the way. Again, like all psychic gifts, divination skills are to be shared with others.

A true psychic doesn't necessarily need the cards to tell them about a person's life and future. They are simply a tool for accessing information and are secondary to the psychic gifts you have. Trust your instincts and eventually you won't even bother looking up the meanings of the cards, you will just trust your clairvoyant skills.

PREPARING TO READ THE CARDS

Before you begin your reading, choose a quiet room and prepare yourself. Do some deep breathing and practise some of the exercises illustrated earlier to prepare yourself to connect with your psychic powers.

If you have invited someone to come and receive a reading from you, remember that they will be nervous. Reassure them that you won't tell them anything that will frighten them and remind them that the things you will say are the potential for the future, not actual fact.

Learn the positions of each lay that you may want to use – there are many. The most well known one is the cross, but experiment to find out how you want to place the cards and how the position occupied by the card influences the reading. Have a lay for specific questions and a longer one for a character reading or life reading.

When your client arrives, ask them not to tell you anything about themselves until you have had a chance to begin the reading. Knowing too much about the person will distract your intuitive flow.

1 Ask your client if there is a specific problem they may want to ask about, or if they would like a general reading.
2 Choose your pack of tarot cards and let the client shuffle them, then lay them out face-down on a table or on the floor.
3 First look at the cards that dominate the reading and bring up the most potent feeling, i.e. what you're getting from your initial reaction to the cards. These pointers indicate which subjects you should be talking about.
4 Look at the individual cards: start each card with an interpretation, feel into the card, the reason why it is in that position and the imagery. Dig deeper for the real significance of why this card has been chosen.

5 Touch the card, close your eyes and watch the images appearing in your mind. Extend your sensing of the meaning, letting yourself go into what you pick up – don't hold back as the cards will tell you lots more than the surface imagery, and your own intuition will tell you even more.

6 As you move through each card, it is like telling the client a story about their life and the people in it.

7 Consider all the other cards and the meaning of the position they occupy before seeing how they relate to each other and their significance. Let your logical mind take a back seat and free your intuition to make the connection between the images and symbols you see before you. Combine this with the psychic impressions that you may be picking up from your client and you will give readings that astound people.

There are many other tools for divination, such as tasseography, the art of reading tea cups. This has been around for centuries. The gypsies have practised the art, the Chinese believe that they invented it, the Romans used to read the residue left over in their wine cups and even Catholic countries such as Ireland have their psychic cup-scrying grandmothers. Cloud reading, palmistry, *I Ching*, astrology, graphology, runes, sand reading, the crystal ball – these are just a few of the thousands of fortune-telling tools. The key to using these tools is to learn how to connect with your psychic sense, and practise with your chosen tool for a period of time. Do this and you can master virtually any oracle.

Psychometry

Some people have referred to psychometry as 'seeing through fingers'. It's all about reading energy vibrations left on objects.

Psychometric vibrations are left on everything: buildings, jewellery, watches; even plants, flowers and crystals – anything that has been absorbing energy from living things. For example, a watch you have worn daily for years will have absorbed your vital energy and within its own vibration will hold yours. Therefore, when a psychic holds your watch they can read your personality by just feeling the vibration.

Objects that we own for a long time absorb vibration – just like buildings and places. Just as the magnetic tape of a cassette recorder has music imprinted on it that can be played back many times, so objects hold 'recordings' of the character, emotions and memories of the owner – and in some cases even those of the maker of the object, particularly if it is a religious or sacred object. A good psychic can read these 'records' of our lives and give a detailed

history of the owner. Sometimes this may include names of family members, friends and places that the owner once knew.

Psychometry teaches you to sense the atmosphere of a place or read the history of an object. An extension of this gift is to sense the atmosphere of a person and become aware of people in the spirit world. Tuning into the energy of a person or place is the first level in learning how to interpret psychic information. When you practise psychometry you will be amazed at how accurate the information that you pick up can be.

Clare, a London-based PA, never considered herself to be psychic. During a psychic awareness workshop she was asked to pick up a ring which belonged to her partner's deceased grandmother. She tuned in to the ring for only a few minutes before the hairs on the back of her neck stood up and she smelt a strong fragrance of perfume (the grandmother's favourite). She surprised herself by opening up to psychic skills she never thought she had. She found out later that her grandmother had a talent for reading signs in tea leaves and had become well known in her village for giving advice and telling the future from what she saw in people's tea cups.

Psychics believe that thought travels outside of the body and is absorbed by our environment. This would account for the sense of atmosphere that is felt in buildings. An ancient church, for example, may feel peaceful and sacred, whilst a stately home, which may be as old as a church, with centuries of activity may have an atmosphere that belies its tragic family history.

Tuning into a place uses the same principles as tuning into a person. As a psychic you are reading into the vibrational energy. Glimpses of history are sometimes a form of psychometry: a psychic inadvertently becomes aware of the atmosphere of a place and suddenly finds themselves replaying images from the past. These visions could be daydreams and fantasy but sometimes a person is psychic enough to be able to see directly into history.

Many researchers believe that ghosts are an etheric imprint left behind by traumatic events. Have you ever walked into a property and felt the atmosphere of the past and even in some cases felt there were ghosts lingering around? These places are very easy to read and are fascinating to use for practising in how to tune into places. This is how I learnt to have confidence in my own skills – by visiting haunted homes and ancient places. I could then follow up my visits with research to find out how accurate my visions and psychic impressions were.

Learning Psychometry

The impressions you receive when doing psychometry will at first come as a flood of mixed messages and images. The first step is to learn how to unravel these and build them into a coherent story. I have trained many talented students who began their training by accurately picking up impressions from people or objects. They were unable, however, to communicate these images in a practical and grounded way until they gained experience and learnt how to communicate their impressions.

Improving Your Psychometric Skills

The key to improving your psychometric skills is to practise on a regular basis. First choose a like-minded friend to work with you on this development. If possible, work from your home. Choose a room where you will not be disturbed, preferably a room with no television or telephone.

Get your friend to choose an object whose origin you are unaware of. Hold the object in the palm of your hand, move it around and touch all the way around the object until you begin to sense an energy or a feeling come over you. Start to talk to them about what you see or feel when you begin to understand what you are picking up and are able to put it in a coherent order.

The impressions that you can pick up from psychometry are limitless. Always structure and keep what you see as practical as possible so the person who you are reading for understands what you are telling them. You may see images that appear not to have any physical relevance, such as an animal or a picture of a sunset or a raging fire. These images could symbolize the person's emotional or spiritual life and indicate an interpretation rather than a prediction.

1 THE OWNER
Talk about the character of the object's owner, how you see them. Just guess and go with your instinct. Are they tall, small, male, female, old or young? The colour of their hair, eyes and any physical disabilities, etc.

2 THE PAST
Next focus on their past – childhood, relationships, family, siblings, and any births or deaths that have ocurred in the family.

3 LIFE HISTORY
Gradually move forward in time and pick up their current profession, emotional relationships, marriages, children, etc.

4 THE PRESENT
Keep going until you reach the present and then describe events that have recently happened, the car they drive, their home, their profession and family life.

Note: when you open up your sensitivity, you must then close down afterwards (see Psychic Protection, pages 92–105).

Images that come through from the psychic realms have their own linear level so it requires a grounded and practical mind to discern all the symbols and images. This takes the most practice, as you need to know when you are actually picking information up or when it is your imagination interpreting something else.

Later, when you learn about the development of other psychic gifts, such as mediumship and clairvoyance, you will understand the importance of getting your impressions into a workable order. The work you do now is the cornerstone of the clear, concise and evidential clairvoyance that marks a good psychic. Students who come to my psychic awareness workshops work hard at developing their psychometric skills so after a few months of laborious practice they are able to move on naturally to reading auras and communicating with the spirit world.

Once you have practised psychometry a few times with familiar people try using it with someone you do not know – this will really test your skill.

Dreaming

The ancient Egyptians and Greeks believed that dreams were messages from the Gods that revealed future events. In many early cultures the term 'incubation' meant seeking information by way of dreams. It was believed that transmitted material from the spirit world was passed into a channel for the recipient to pick up while they were dreaming. However, as this material is incorporated into the dream, the dreamer must recognize it as such and decipher it before waking.

Dreams contain prophecies and are an important key to self-knowledge. Known as the gateway to psychic powers, dreams are our means of bringing spiritual information and intuition from our higher self into our consciousness. We dream every night and, whether we remember them or not, our dreams reveal our innermost desires. They can also be used to solve difficult problems. The dream state allows the brain to interpret the events of the day: it digests the information we have received and, free from the constraints of our conscious mind, can solve issues, worries and fears and, occasionally, tell us about the future. Nightmares in particular provide important clues about fears and problems and recalling them, however scary, can help release these emotions.

Thoughts, ideas, worries, hopes and fears are all represented by symbols, metaphors and images within our dreams. The subconscious mind draws from our experiences and writes them into a mini play. Most of us are emotionally at the mercy of our worries and troubles, but if we use dreams properly we can, with a little effort, become the master of ourselves and learn how to connect with our psychic powers.

Using Dreams as a Psychic Connection

To become more aware of your dreams, try setting your alarm clock slightly earlier than usual. With luck, you will interrupt a dream that has something to say about you, or your future – even offer a solution to a problem that you may be experiencing.

Dreams can be excellent problem solvers. Write down your problem in the form of a question. Then, just before you go to sleep, put it under your pillow and affirm in your head what you have written down. Try to see the question in a picture form rather than in words. Pray to your inner self to help find a solution – once you have set the programme running, your dreams should do the rest. If you find that you get no answer the first night, affirm your question over seven nights and then check if you have dreamt the answer. Many people find that the dream doesn't mean anything until something happens in their day to remind them of the dream – only then does the answer come.

Keeping a Dream Diary

Most dreams are forgotten in 10 minutes, so to remember them just run through the dream in your mind before you get up, then write it down straight away. Don't worry about how you write it: sometimes you may want to draw what you saw – it is not an essay, it is a diary to help you interpret messages from your subconscious. Even if you didn't dream, write down the first thoughts you had as this may trigger recall.

List everything, no matter how unimportant it may seem. Note the day and time and divide the paper into two – in one column write down or draw your dream, and in the other write your interpretation. The key is how you interpret your dreams and the symbolism within them. For instance, once you have written the dream down, pay attention not just to how you felt about the dream, but to the way you describe it, the references you make, the turns of phrase, and any memories it may trigger – they are all clues to the answer your dream is providing. You will get flashbacks to your dream throughout the day, note these as some will help solve problems or missing links.

If you work at unravelling your own dream symbols, you will eventually find that the images speak for themselves. In the majority of dream interpretation books you will find that there are links to typical emotional reactions. For example, teeth falling out in a dream indicates insecurity and in some books means that a part of your self is dying. Water relates to emotions, fire to anger or passion, and so on. Most dreams don't fit neatly into categories – they are your own unique experience – but a good dream analysis book and some interesting dream imagery will keep you fascinated for a long time and will help in your personal psychic development.

Spirit Communication

Many psychics believe that they are guided by personalities in spirit who are able to offer valuable information and support through clairaudience, clairvoyance, clairsentience and channelling. Some believe that their guides are people who were once physically alive and who now inhabit a higher spiritual dimension. In some cases, their guides may be known; relatives, friends or former partners who continue to offer guidance to the people they love beyond the limits of their physical mortality. Others, subscribing to a belief in reincarnation, claim that in psychic intervention their spirit guides take the form of personalities they once knew in a former life.

The types of psychics who communicate with spirits are channels or mediums. The word channel appears to come from the US and covers a broad spectrum of psychic abilities and creative talents. Any of us can be said to be channelling when we lose ourselves to a creative process, whether it is painting a picture, writing a book, dancing, singing or chanting.

A medium is someone who acts as a vehicle for family or friends wishing to communicate from the spirit realms. Many psychics and mediums channel guidance or information in the form of mental pictures (clairvoyance), hearing subtle sounds or words (clairaudience) and in the form of sound and smell (clairsentience). A lot of material is also channelled in the form of automatic writing; this tends to be from information given by spirit guides and teachers.

There is no great mystery in communicating with Spirit; we are all capable of learning this skill. It is also possible to learn how to channel positive inspirational guidance to help others. (Refer to the chapter on spirit communication for practical guidance on how to communicate with Spirit and meet your spirit guides.)

Clairsentience

This is frequently defined as the ability to sense psychical manifestations that cannot be perceived by any of our five senses. It is the power to sense the atmosphere of a house or place; to know that there is a psychic manifestation. This ability is akin to psychometry and can show itself as a general uneasiness, a distinct feeling of coldness, negativity, even the prickling of hairs on the back of the neck or down the arm.

The majority of clairsentience experiences are spontaneous as it is often dependent on the way we tune into places and into the essences of people's personalities. The most common example of tuning into a place is an ability to sense a strange atmosphere in a house as soon as one enters it. It is also common to discover a scent that comes from the spirit world. This is the first entry point into clairsentience and indeed is often the way people sense either the deceased or the history of a place. For example, smelling a deceased grandmother's favourite perfume or baking or a grandfather's tobacco is a universal paranormal phenomena. A few years ago I had a spirit guide from India and when he came to visit there was always a strong smell of jasmine in the room.

Clairsentience is the first opening from being intuitive or sensitive to describing yourself as psychic. We have all experienced times when our intuition is acute and we are able to listen to it and respond accordingly. Your intuition tells you that it would be a good time to telephone a friend; you have a 'gut feeling' she is in need of support and it turns out she is. Clairsentience is particularly common in women and children, who are still generally more emotionally biased than men. As children we are all quite open intuitively and emotionally; if you watch small children react to people and situations that they feel uncomfortable with or do not like, they are reacting to a feeling that they receive from that situation or person. However, as we grow we may learn to shut out these aspects of our awareness. To be clairsentient is to be as sensitive to situations and people as a small child, and to listen to those feelings and trust them.

Clairsentience is a very important skill because it offers protection, not only against bad vibrations from a haunted place, but also against present dangers or potential hostility.

I have never questioned my sensitivity to atmospheres since an event that happened when I was 19. One Saturday night I had gone to a party with a small group of friends. We were sitting in the living room when I experienced a terrible cold feeling in my stomach and insisted

to my friends that we had to leave (this is before I trained in psychic development!). Reluctantly, my friends left with me and as we were walking out we came across a group of rough-looking youths waiting to come in. The next day I discovered that one of the youths had stabbed a guest who had been sitting where we had been. I sensed danger and thank God I listened to my feelings.

Intuitive responses tell us that a stranger is untrustworthy, even though their outer appearance or actions offer no apparent justification for this distrust. This automatic response is in-built in us all, but too often we don't recognize our natural warning system. Dogs will growl at some apparently friendly strangers but not at others, while a normally confident child will sometimes instinctively back away from a smile and outstretched hand. In both cases, the person usually proves to be unreliable or to have negative intentions behind the smile and soft words. This is the same intuitive ability that makes us instantly like or dislike a place, a person or a situation.

This skill is more open in some people than others, particularly if they have more of an emotional outlook on life. Those who approach life with a more mental and visual outlook will lean more towards clairvoyance.

Clairvoyance

We often dismiss our psychic abilities by telling ourselves that we are imagining things. Many of us regard our imagination as something that is unreal or illusory. A well-developed imagination, however, is very important for our psychic development as it provides us with an effective bridge to valuable psychic information, as well as an abundance of creative energy. To develop psychically you need to give yourself permission to dream, to fantasize and play, before allowing the rational mind to do the necessary job of sorting out and assessing how to act upon the information that you receive.

The most commonly used term for a psychic is clairvoyant. This term is used to describe someone who gives psychic readings on a professional basis. Clairvoyance describes a range of psychic abilities based on the ability to visualize – to have 'clear sight' or 'clear vision'. A true clairvoyant will receive messages or information through a heightened visual awareness.

A person with developed clairvoyant abilities has a strong sense of inner vision and is able to receive information in the form of visual images or symbols. Most clairvoyants receive their information internally; some describe having something akin to a cinema screen inside their head with images moving across it. Others receive individual symbols that they learn to interpret. Some clairvoyants receive their information externally. This usually means they are able to see people or animals in spirit, or can observe the subtle energy that circulates around themselves when they walk into the room.

Similar to people with a profound psychic ability in other areas, many clairvoyants will have a range of other psychic skills such as clairaudience and clairsentience, but their predominant source of information will tend to be visual.

Subjective Clairvoyance

This is by far the most common form of clairvoyance. Most of us have had the experience of conjuring up an image in our mind's eye when we are remembering a past event or when we are asked to imagine something we have not seen first-hand. Many clairvoyants receive information in a similar fashion, perceiving visual images, symbols and impressions within their mind's eye and then interpreting them accordingly.

These visions come through the third eye, which is one of the seven main chakras (see the chapter on chakras, pages 50–66). Some of the messages come in the form of lights, colours, cinematic images or abstract symbols, seen or perceived in the area of the forehead between and slightly above the eyebrows. Like all psychics, subjective clairvoyants receive information from their own higher mind, spirit guides, visiting spirits from clients that come for a reading, environmental influences and numerous other sources.

Because many clairvoyants receive psychic information in the form of symbols and abstract images, it takes time and practice to be able to interpret these images accurately and with some kind of practical and obvious relation to the person to whom you are giving the information. The images could relate to past lives, telepathic communication, picking up underlying life goals or life purpose, aspects of healing, and overall spiritual development – as well as numerous other issues such as current relationships and work problems.

Interpretation is something to be learned over time and is not something that is easily taught. There is no clairvoyant symbol that has a set meaning or that can be interpreted using a standard formula. Ultimately we are our own best teachers – by trusting what we feel, risking making mistakes and practising as much as we can.

Objective Clairvoyance

Objective clairvoyants are psychics who have the rare talent of being able to see objects, animals and people in spirit as if they were present. While the subjective clairvoyant may get a clear picture of an object internally, the objective clairvoyant sees things in the environment around them. In some cases these things can be quite three dimensional, like looking at things through our physical eyes rather than through our third eye. However, what is happening is that the psychic activity in the third eye is more heightened and active than in a person with subjective clairvoyance. Objective clairvoyance is a talent that tends to be inherited.

Clairvoyant skills are necessary to be able to divine the future, see auras and communicate with spirits.

Clairaudience

Both psychometry and clairsentience skills can trigger clairaudience – the ability to hear words or sounds that are not part of the material world but come from the ether and spirit realms. When developing spirit communication skills, clairaudience is one of the first major steps in communicating with spirits and hearing their voices.

Many people who have natural clairaudience skills will hear spirits and ghosts. As you become increasingly psychically aware, it becomes easier to pick up different frequencies – much as an experienced radio operator can tune a radio more accurately. A frequently reported clairaudient experience is that of hearing footsteps in an otherwise empty house. As with spirit voices, these sounds can exist independently of the hearer and may be heard by several people who live in the house – although they may not all hear them at the same time.

Many people have a degree of clairaudience but do not recognize it as such because, like so many other psychic abilities, it is has always been there. We may have always received words, thoughts or sounds of inspiration inside our mind without ever assuming that they come from another source. Many clairaudient psychics hear psychically transmitted sounds and spoken language as if they were hearing them physically. Others hear or receive the impressions of sounds, words or thoughts only in their minds. Many of our spirit guides and ancestors speak to us through clairaudience and many of the best solutions to our day-to-day problems are received from clairaudient messages. (In section two you will find a number of exercises that help tune your clairaudient and clairvoyant skills.)

Awakening your psychic powers

Most people are psychic to some degree. However, everyone has different gifts and different ways of working with their psychic powers. Psychic energy is not a commodity or something you gain as a result of passing an exam – it is something we all possess. Most people use their intuitive gift or sixth sense without being aware of it. Learning about your gift increases your capacity to use it and by trying out various methods of psychic sensitivity – such as psychometry or fortune telling – you will discover your natural gift. Whichever gift comes naturally is the one you should develop.

To be a successful psychic you need to be interested in people, to believe that there is life after death, and that the power and love within the spiritual world influences the living. Before all these things mean anything to you, you must first learn to understand your own spiritual belief system a little better. Some people are naturally more in touch with themselves and the principles behind their way of bringing a spiritual understanding into their life on a daily basis.

The key to learning how to open up and discover your natural psychic gifts lies in knowing how you feel about yourself and in being conscious of the world you exist in. I always ask my students on the first day of a psychic awareness workshop questions such as: 'How do you treat yourself? Do you eat well, rest and relax? How much do you enjoy your day-to-day life? How successful do you feel about what you have achieved in your life? Are you able to love, care and give without expecting anything in return?'

Do It Yourself Psychic Power

Being a psychic is a difficult gift to live with, although there are many plus points to having a vision of the future and being able to see through people and situations at a glance. To really benefit from being psychic takes time and experience. The happier you are with your life the better, as the best psychics are those who are not afraid of loving, of giving and of being themselves in any given situation.

The gift of psychic power generally begins to appear in people during childhood, though this is not always the case. Many people have opened themselves up in adulthood: some after a traumatic experience, others following a near-death experience and some through many years of training.

There are many ways to uncover your talents. Many of the strands of psychic powers are interlinked and the more you experiment, the further your psychic powers will unfold and evolve. However, in order to become aware of your psychic power, and to be able to tune into people, vibrations and atmospheres, it is essential to learn how to meditate.

Meditation and Self-awareness

'Meditating using simple yoga-style meditation techniques has helped me to transform my brain activity from conscious reality into a higher, unconscious reality. I can feel myself connect with my spirit and gradually I move into my inner space and connect up with the creator spirit.'
Florence, French language teacher

Meditation is a discipline that encourages your mind to focus and to interpret psychic visions, messages and symbols from the spirit world. It also encourages confidence in your psychic abilities.

There is a multitude of meditation techniques. The purpose in most traditional forms is to move us closer to spiritual liberation, closer to a unity with a divine force. In general, the very idea of moving closer to the source of 'great' spirituality can put the majority of people off ever learning how to meditate. However, if we view it as a simple exercise that takes our focus away from the physical reality into an inner peaceful space, then we may approach it with less trepidation.

Through meditation we can free our thoughts, though to achieve this requires patience and perseverance. Initially, it is hard to halt the continuous chatter that goes on in the mind.

Meditation is like taming a wild animal; at first it will be moving around wildly, not wanting to be still. You cannot force it to be still, eventually it will simply tire and look for a place to rest. Your technique will become a place on which your mind rests. Each time you meditate the mind will remain focused for longer periods and even when distracted will easily return to the focus point.

Meditation is an excellent way of taking a break from the external world and going on an inner journey. In this way it is possible to attain great insight into the nature of one's self – a process which can, of course, bring both pain and joy. It can help uncover facets of our character that we don't like or experiences we have repressed, but it can also in time bring us to a place of surrender where a state of grace or union with God can occur. In Indian Yogic terms this is called *Samadhi* – a state of bliss or peace.

The benefits of meditation are not only mental but physical. It involves deep physical relaxation and affects respiration, making it slower and deeper. The pulse rate also slows and muscular activity lessens. Through meditation you start to see things differently and have more clarity. The outside pressures of your daily life may not change but your view of them shifts, you feel stronger but calmer, relaxed, less tense and more able to cope with the stresses of daily life.

It is impossible to convey the reality of meditation through words alone. Meditation can only be understood through direct experience. Meditation can be viewed as a state of consciousness or a way of life. It might be seen as a path to enlightenment and a spiritual discipline. It is all things to all people.

Prayer

Prayer is a form of meditation, a means of connecting with the inner spirit. Most of us have prayed at some point in our lives, in particular in times of need and desperation, or when giving thanks or seeking guidance.

Prayer is personal and a direct communication with our creator. It reminds us that we are not alone; there is a greater power, a natural force that guides and protects our every move, that governs the cycles of life and the ebb and flow of human existence. Sometimes we need to 'learn' to surrender and let these forces guide us. Once we have experienced a moment of spiritual security or a connection with the divine we know it exists. The next step is to encourage that relationship to enable 'it' to be a part of our daily life.

Morning Prayer

Light a candle on your altar each morning on rising. Then take a few moments to give thanks and to ask for guidance. You can use traditional prayer or open your heart and let your own words flow freely. Be mindful and open to your prayers being answered – and be careful for what you ask for. Repeat the process before going to bed.

Preparation for Meditation

Your Environment

Practise in a quiet room that is warm and well aired – preferably the room where you have your altar (see page 143). Create a calming atmosphere by lighting candles and burning incense or essential oils. If possible, meditate in the same room each day. This will lift the vibrations in the space, aiding your spiritual and psychic connection considerably. It is important to make this space a sanctuary for your meditations, a place where you can enjoy the process of meditation and easily connect to your sacred observances (see The Sanctuary, page 140).

Timing

Try to practise your meditation at the same time every day. This will attune your personal energy and encourage meditation to become a habit. The amount of time that people spend meditating varies. When you first begin to meditate you may find that just 5 minutes twice a day or 10 minutes once a day is enough. This may not sound a lot but you will be surprised at just how difficult it is to meditate without being interrupted by your thoughts – if you can manage 20 seconds when you first begin you're doing pretty well! If you try to meditate for too long before you're ready you're in danger of turning the process into a chore. Decide on the amount of time you wish to spend meditating and stick to it. You can increase the time as and when you feel happy – but keep it consistent, not 5 minutes one day and 15 the next.

Relaxation Before Meditation

Before meditation practice some people need to first relax their bodies. This can be done in various ways: taking physical exercise, doing a yoga or tai chi class, or focusing on the rise and fall of the breath. Another popular way to wind down is having a candle-lit bath with your favourite essential oils.

Physical Position

Posture is very important in meditation. One should feel relaxed but not sleepy, so an upright sitting position is best. There are several positions to use: sitting cross-legged on the floor, sitting on a dining chair or kneeling, whichever is most comfortable for you. The most important thing is for the spine to be relaxed but erect. Keeping the spine straight assists the channelling of energy from the mind through into the body. Another important aspect is comfort; if you are not comfortable and warm during meditation you will tend to lose concentration and focus more on trying to obtain a comfortable position than on meditating.

Mental Outlook

Prepare your mind to accept the duration of meditation and ask your mind to be silent throughout the meditation practice. I find that if I concentrate on my breath and tell my mind to focus on my breathing after the next thought, that this slows the process of connecting one thought after another (the function of the conscious mind). Meditation allows the connection with the higher conscious mind to filter its peaceful stillness into our conscious state. This slows down the thoughts, creating a space between each one – and this is the beginning of meditation.

Breathing

Before you attempt to meditate, spend a few minutes consciously regulating your breath. Use your nose not your mouth when taking an in-breath, and try to breath out of your nose not your mouth. Take several deep abdominal breaths. The stomach should be pushed out on your in-breath and return towards the spine on the out-breath. Try to keep your shoulders relaxed and neck straight with the chin tucked in slightly towards the chest. Each breath you take should be slow and rhythmic.

The following techniques can be used prior to meditation (or at at any other time) to relax the body and mind.

Breathing Exercises

- Concentrate on taking in a deep breath to fill your lungs and chest fully, count to seven as you breathe in, hold your breath for three counts, then take a long deep out-breath to the count of seven. Repeat this action seven times.

- Begin with the breathing sequence above, then take your concentration from your breath and imagine you are blowing energy into your feet, then up your legs, into your pelvis, through your solar plexus into your heart, throat, shoulders, neck, face, head and down the spine back into your feet. As you gently breathe in imagine you are breathing in light and then breathe out this light into your body. Repeat three times. This technique moves the breath through your physical body, sending the power of breath into each muscle, bone, nerve ending and organ.

Meditation Exercises

After you have calmed your mind with your breath you may begin your chosen meditation. Two basic types of meditation technique are generally taught today. The first is the Zen approach of 'silent sitting': in this method you sit facing a blank wall or mirror until the mind becomes blank. In psychic development groups, candlelight or a crystal is often used instead. The idea is to sit until the moment of pure enlightenment happens, even if it takes twenty years. The second approach uses a mantra; a sound or image that rhythmically lulls the mind into quietness. After a thousand repetitions the body begins to vibrate at a higher frequency and the meditator becomes aware of higher energies beyond the physical senses of our daily mind.

There are numerous meditation exercises that I would recommend, for instance:

- Focusing on the light of a candle
- Concentrating on a picture of the chakra symbols
- Concentrating on a picture of a deity (god or goddess)
- Focusing on the point between your eyebrows, the third eye
- Chakra meditation

Staring at a candle flame is often used to prepare a psychic in a development class. The candle is placed reasonably close to the eyes, letting the mind connect with the image to build up an interpretation of psychic imaging. The same technique is also used with symbols and other images, as well as flowers, crystals, colours and even sand.

When we first begin meditating, however, the aim is to still the mind; not to follow the endless chatter that it throws up. In this way we begin to open up space in our mind – we do away with the superficial and create space for the psychic and spiritual.

Counting your Breath

This is a popular meditation technique with beginners, as focusing on the breath is easier than the more 'passive' staring techniques.

• Sit in your meditation position, relax and focus on your breathing – do not try to control it, simply observe it.

• Now begin to count your breaths. Count one inhale and exhale as one. The aim is simply to count the breaths without letting other thoughts intervene. Count up to ten. If a train of thought makes you lose count, go back to one again.

Third Eye Meditation

This meditation is for the more advanced student.

• Sit in your meditation position, relax and focus on your breathing – do not try to control it, simply observe it.

• Now take your attention to the third eye between your eyebrows. Close your eyes and focus on the third eye centre. Just as you observed your breath, do the same with your mind. Do not follow any thoughts that come into your mind, simply watch them and let them go by. If you find that you have slipped and fallen into a stream of thinking, bring yourself back to the third eye centre and start again.

Through meditation, thoughts can turn into visions. Some may be beautiful and others ugly. Treat them all with the same detachment. Observe them and let them go. Many will be of a psychic nature – such as visions, prophecies or glimpses of things happening in other places – but, for the time being, let these go also. Focus on being an unattached observer.

By separating yourself from your thinking, you attune yourself with what mystics call the 'overself', our higher consciousness. This extends into the spirit world and beyond. You may experience being the watcher of yourself in your day-to-day life, becoming closer to the realization of the true nature of the self within your personality.

Meditation exercises are a starting point for the greater inner awareness essential to a healthy psychic connection. By opening the third eye centre you have taken the first serious steps to true clairvoyance. But remember – it takes a lot of patience and regular practice to open yourself to your psychic gifts. (For in-depth books on meditation see Resources section, page 180).

Techniques for Tuning into and Focusing your Psychic Vision

When we have learnt how to calm mind and body, we need to learn how to tune in and listen to our inner voice. We begin this process by connecting with our personal sacredness – through spending time in nature.

When I first learnt how to meditate, my psychic development teacher insisted that I spent time in nature, listening to and feeling the seasons, the birdsong – even watching the clouds go by. It was the first time as an adult that I had been given permission to just be still. This was alien to me at first, but I soon realized the benefits. My psychic technique improved considerably – I learnt how to be still so it became easier to tune in and listen to Spirit.

Meditating in Nature

Meditation and connecting with your inner space is not just about sitting in quiet concentration, central as this is to meditation practice. It is also about a range of active techniques that enhance the powers of mind control. These powers are used not only while sitting in meditation but also in our day-to-day lives and even while we dream. Meditation thus touches most aspects of human experience, rendering them potentially richer, more profound and more meaningful.

Learning to tune into the energy outside yourself is not difficult; the energy sources are all around us in nature and nature speaks to us at all times, it's just that we seldom listen.

Nature Meditation

If you listen to the sound of nature – if you tap into the earth's powerful energy – you will hear messages that have the power to uplift and transform you. Try these simple methods of tuning into the earth. When done mindfully, these exercises will resonate at a deeper level.

- Watch the clouds while lying on the ground
- Watch a sunset and sunrise and be inspired
- As night falls catch the first star
- Enjoy a summer evening in your garden watching the sun set and the moon rise
- Sit alone in a tree and feel the wind brush across your face
- Stand alone on a hill top
- Sit on the sea shore or by a lake and watch the water

The list is endless, but when was the last time that you enjoyed being in nature? It is an invaluable way of connecting with your sense of wholeness and being restored by the power within the earth.

'Wherever I am in the world I try to connect at the same time each day to meditate and open my spirit to the divine. I ask for help and offer prayers for world issues and my family. On some days I conduct a ritual, I celebrate an event in my life or connect with God for healing and upliftment.' Susan, ballet dancer and teacher

Morning Connection Meditation

It is important to start every day by connecting with a deeper aspect of your self and the best way to do this is by having a morning ritual. This puts you in harmony with your surroundings and prepares you to face everyone you meet during your day with equanimity. Try it for a week and watch the difference in your confidence and energy levels

Morning Ritual

To conduct your ritual, ideally you should get up an hour earlier to give yourself a clear period of connecting time each day. The more you practise the less time it takes – my ritual now takes 20–30 minutes.

1 As you emerge from your night's sleep catch some of the inspiration from your sleep. You can do this by saying a morning prayer to your god, guides and spirit deities.

2 Warm up your body by taking a hot drink (whatever your favourite morning drink is – mine is hot water and lemon juice).

3 Do a few minutes of physical exercise – either yoga (sun salutation is ideal), tai chi, qi gong or even a few aerobic stretches (whatever your favourite exercise is) – to encourage your body to loosen up, realign your spine, stimulate your internal organs, balance your energy and clear your mind.

4 Now begin your meditation exercises.

5 Finish with a prayer to your spirit guides and deities for peace and protection – or whatever the day requires. I like to light a candle at my altar and read a few lines from a spiritually inspiring book to get me in the mood for the day. I sometimes choose an oracle or tarot card to show me how the day will flow; at other times it will be the magical little angel cards to get me in a higher frame of mind. I leave the cards on my altar to give their energy to my day.

6 I complete the ritual by calling Spirit for protection, and wrap up in a psychic cloak to protect my aura (see page 97).

• Warning: You will get good days and terrible ones but you should do the morning ritual every day regardless, unless you are ill.

Clearing Your Energy

At the end of each day spend 10 minutes clearing your energy and your mind. One of the simplest ways to do this is to have a candle-lit bath with uplifting and calming aromatherapy oils such as chamomile, rose, lavender or geranium. Other recommended practices for cleansing your energy include breathing exercises, smudging your aura with a sage stick, yoga, tai chi, qi gong exercises and chakra-clearing exercises (see pages 62–66).

Grounding Meditation

This meditation is a deeper alternative to the daily morning ritual, as it connects your mind, body and spirit to the earth. This aim is to ground your spiritual energies and open your mind both to a wider vision for your day and to receive creative inspiration. I find that working with nature gives me a lot of creative and spiritual power.

Choose a tall, ancient tree in a field or copse as the focal point for this meditation.

1 Start by sitting or standing with an erect spine against the tree trunk and imagine your spine and the tree melding into one energy. This is a meeting with tree power and earth energy.

2 Through the roots of the tree – which are linked to the nervous system within our feet – the power of the earth can be drawn up into the spine. As the power rises it is drawn up inside us to touch the heavens, connecting the earth and sky. With the meeting of these opposites a restfulness and peace enters the spine.

3 Breathing gently, permit your thoughts to move away from the mind as body, mind and spirit are regenerated.

Once the connection has been made an earth ritual may be conducted. A ritual is a sacred act; a celebration acknowledging that there is a life power, which we honour by the giving of gifts to the spirit of place. The gifts may change according to the customs of the culture/country. For instance in Celtic countries the land is honoured by gifts of food or alcohol. A personal gesture made with heartfelt intentions would make the ritual a personal tribute to the earth. Bringing a candle or gifts of flowers would also make the ritual blessed to honour the vision which may be received by connecting to this earth power.

You can also conduct the same meditation using a standing stone. Here the energy is drawn directly into the spine and fills each bone in your body. A similar meditation can be conducted in a cave, by a cliff, on a stony beach – or you can hold a stone in your hand and meditate with it.

Psychic Development Exercises

When you have become adept at the practice of meditation and are applying meditation on a daily basis, it's time to work on opening your mind through psychic development exercises.

You will need to try these out a few times before you get the hang of how they improve your psychic technique. Practise them for a month, then leave it for a month before returning to the exercises to see if you have improved your focus.

Imagery

To learn how to work with your psychic senses, you first need to develop the discipline to be able to see clearly the images that you may pick up when working with your psychic vision. These practises are simple and, when worked at on a daily basis, strengthen your abilities. It takes about 20 minutes to do all three sections and they should be practised on a daily basis until your mind becomes fluid enough to pick up strong imagery.

Using Your Inner Senses

You need to do these while by yourself, anywhere that is comfortable for you.

VISUAL
Form the following images in your mind's eye:

- Your name written on a piece of paper
- Your date of birth in numbers
- A bright red square
- A bright green circle
- A star
- A candle flame

AUDITORY
Recreate the following sounds in your inner ear imagination:

- The sound of someone you know calling your name
- Children playing in a school playground
- A church bell
- Busy traffic
- A train
- The sound of the sea crashing on rocks

KINESTHETIC (MOVEMENT)
Sense your movements and imagine yourself doing the following:

- Walking
- Running
- Swimming
- Dancing
- Kicking a football
- Making a bed

I have found that the older I get the more dense my imagination. It isn't as free and vivid as it once was and I have to move the grey fog out of the way before the stronger, more vibrant images come into focus. These exercises help keep my mind focused.

Using Touch, Taste and Smell

Now we are going to take it a step further and work with your touch, taste and smell.

TACTILE
Sense yourself doing the following:

- Touching the rough bark of a tree
- Stroking a cat
- Placing your hand under running water
- Shaking hands
- Placing your hand in snow and feeling it go numb
- Delicately touching the petal of a rose

GUSTATORY
Sense what it's like to taste the following:

- Salted peanuts
- Your favourite dessert
- A hot drink
- Ice-cream
- A hot chilli dish
- A piece of your favourite fruit

OLFACTORY
Sense what it's like to smell the following:

- Your favourite perfume
- Freshly baking bread
- A bunch of flowers
- Petrol
- A joss stick
- Mint

The next series of exercises develops your intuitive understanding through body awareness – the part of us that responds to emotions and feelings. This discipline enables you to clearly understand when your body is saying yes and when it is responding with a no. Since running workshops I have realized that many people don't always understand their body responses – whether to food, drink or to situations. We don't always listen to ourselves. Working with these simple suggestions can open your understanding of how your body responds to various situations.

Intuiting Yes and No Through Body Awareness

WHEN YOU SENSE YOUR BODY IS SAYING YES

Imagine something you love to do, such as eating your favourite food or soaking in a hot bath or lying on a sun-kissed beach. Focus on your body sensations as you do this. The sensations will give you a sense of how your body conveys 'yes' to you.

WHEN YOU SENSE YOUR BODY IS SAYING NO

Focus on the sensations in your body when you imagine somebody calling you by the wrong name or you imagine yourself eating a food you dislike, or your bath water being too cold when you step into it. The sensations will give you a sense of how your body conveys 'no' to you.

Below are some descriptions of people's responses to the exercise.

YES responses are as follows:

Feeling open and expanded
Clarity
Lightness
Peace
Relaxation
Warm glow
Happy and all-embracing
Safe and calm

NO responses are as follows:

Scrunched in the solar plexus
Contracted
Heaviness and cloudiness
Painful
Twisted
Pressure
Closing down
Dark and sad

Once your have learnt your 'yes' and 'no' responses practise tuning in to your body when you are in your day-to-day life and see how your body is responding then.

Preparing to do Psychic Work

As you become involved in psychic work you will find you have difficulty deciding whether you are actually sensing these realities or just imagining them. This goes hand in hand with confusion about how you perceive psychic imagery. In actual fact, the way that most of us perceive atmospheres and vibrations is through feeling and sensing them. Learning to differentiate between when you are experiencing a psychic atmosphere or when you are simply responding to your own vibrations takes time and practice. This next set of exercises will help you tune yourself into working in a psychic capacity. They prepare your mind and body, so they should be practised just before you conduct any psychic work. Eventually you will be able to connect with your psychic powers automatically.

Take a few minutes to work through each exercise, beginning each one slowly until you understand what it is doing to your mind and body.

Before doing inner work you must learn to relax. Try the following:

- Let go of any tightness or tension in your muscles
- Sigh on your out-breath
- Do an inner smile

Tuning In

If you are familiar with the chakras then open the chakras through a visualization technique before you begin these exercises. If not, refer to page 100 where there is an exercise on opening and closing the chakras.

BECOME AWARE OF STILLNESS AND PEACE
Become aware of your breathing, notice that moment of stillness just at the end of your out-breath and for that moment allow your mind and emotions to be equal, in a place of stillness. Repeat seven times.

CENTRING
Imagine breathing in through your crown and out through your base. Then in through your base and out through your crown; sense that central column of energy within your body.

PROTECTIVE GOLDEN OR WHITE LIGHT
Imagine golden or white light coming in through your crown and going right through to the tips of your fingers and the tips of your toes. Then imagine this light glowing brighter and brighter until it creates a wonderful cushion of energy all around you.

GROUNDING
Imagine roots going out from under your feet deep into the core of the earth, or a taproot growing out of the base of your spine and into the core of the earth.

CLEANSING
Imagine you are under a shower or waterfall of sparkling golden water, being cleansed inside and out, as you let go of anything that is upsetting or bothering you.

INVOKING A HIGHER POWER OF LOVE AND LIGHT
In a prayer or chant say 'I invite my Higher Self, the light and creation, my healing guides and angels to be here with me, so I experience all the insight and healing that is most appropriate for me now under guidance of my Higher Self and my God.'

Closing Down

When your energy centres are open, you are in an interactive exchange with the environment around you, both physical and psychic. Whenever you have completed a psychic connection you must close down your energy field by closing down the chakras. So if you have envisioned the chakras as flowers you must see the petals close and if you envision them as doors then they must be closed. (See Psychic Protection, pages 92–105.)

Sacred Time

Everything in nature is rhythm. Everything in the universe is in motion; nothing is fixed, permanent, unchanging. This eternal pulse is in everything – sound, breath, light and vibration. To become aware of these cyclic rhythms to which our body, mind and spirit are subjected to is learning how to swim with the rhythm not against it.

The sun and the moon were regarded among ancient peoples as representative of the duality of the masculine and feminine principles inherent in nature, and of the active and passive, conceptual and receptive forces that permeate it. They used these forces to create a rhythm and cycle for spiritual life.

Timing is an important element in the practice of psychic awareness and connection with the sacred. So are some times better than others? There are many factors that influence psychic powers and spiritual connection. The three most important ones are:

- The different energy of the day and of the night
- The times when day and night meet
- The phases of the moon

In setting aside time to connect you will need to take care of your practical and immediate needs and obligations. It is important that you dedicate a specific time each day or each week to practise.

Creating a habit or ritual in your routine enables your mind and body to become accustomed to that time to tune in, and this regularity of connection creates confidence in tuning into your psychic powers. It won't work, however, if you decide that you want to create a sacred moment when your children are screaming, or if it makes you late for the office. It is better to dedicate only an hour a week to your psychic practice, if during that time you can be serene and enjoy connecting, than to try to greet the day with a full ceremonial ritual when you're pushed for time.

Day Time

During the day the energy of the sun is predominant. It is strong, active and expanding. Sunshine 'draws you out' and empowers energy; it makes you want to explore and try new things, it gives you courage, and helps communication, business and commerce. It is the Yang (male) energy of Chinese philosophy.

Day time furthers psychic powers that involve relating to others, expanding in the world, and gaining strength and power. Work and money are dealt with best during the day, as are matters of travel and the blossoming stages of a love affair.

Night Time

During the night the moon is queen. Her energy is cool and soft, receptive, introspective and mysterious. Night time furthers meditation and silence, and creative inspiration in pursuits such as poetry and art. It is the Yin (female) energy of Chinese philosophy.

Rituals aimed at discovering some hidden truth within ourselves should be conducted at night, as should absent healing, astral travel and any psychic communication with another who is far away. Divination is usually performed during these hours and supernatural experiences are at their most potent. Fertility and creativity are for the night, while prosperity and focus are day-time magic.

Sunrise and Sunset

When night and day meet, at sunrise and sunset, is when miracles can happen. These times should be treasured for making rituals and ceremonies, powerful meditations with the chakras and healing energy.

Have you ever stayed awake all night and watched the darkness retreat into misty forms and colours, and the first rays of the sun break through bursting everything into subtle life? You cannot fail to notice the magical quality of these elemental moments. Such moments help you realize your connection with the night and the powers that you have within you; powers that can be unlocked through this experience reflected by the burst of light that comes at dawn.

SUNRISE

All kinds of rituals can benefit greatly by being performed during sunrise. It is an especially appropriate time for meditations, incantations and asking for specific blessings for new beginnings – for instance finding a new love, a new job or even a new direction in life. Sunrise is better celebrated outside or in some way connected with nature, such as sitting on your patio or balcony, or in front of an open window. Remember to face east, for the east sees the rising of the sun.

SUNSET

Sunset is an equally magical time. It is very common to feel a sudden and poignant sadness or disturbance in your energy/emotions as the light fades into darkness and the day is gone. If you are in a receptive mood, every sunset can be like a small death – the moment to render your accounts and become aware of how you have spent your energies. With the advent of electricity sunset has lost most of its impact. Overshadowed by the glare of artificial lights, the sun sets totally unobserved by the majority of people – unless you make a point of watching it.

Yet sunset is an important time, one of the best moments to feel inside and get to know yourself a little deeper. During times of confusion and stress it is a fruitful moment to contemplate or meditate on your problems; a time when you can view them from a different perspective. The power of the last rays of the sun will give you the energy to connect with the truth about whatever you are seeking answers to.

Midday and Midnight

When the sun is at its highest in the sky, this is the time to use its power in full. Use it for vigour, strength and health, and to give an extra burst of energy to any kind of psychic connection. The darkest hour, midnight, is for banishing magic or rituals. If there is anything your want to get rid of – an attitude, a habit, an idea, something that you wish to be gone from your life – midnight is the time to do it.

Moontime

For millions of years the moon – a bare spherical chunk of rock, solitary and unwavering – has circled the earth, turning its dark side towards us at the new moon and illuminating the night sky at the full moon.

It is well known that the influence of the moon is a very important element in the fluctuations of psychic energy. With the same power that the moon has to raise the tides of the sea, the moon plays upon human souls – especially women, who, since the beginning of time, have learned to recognize the ways and powers of the moon and how to use them. The gravitational force of the moon affects every point on the earth and therefore every human being, every animal, every plant and every atom on our planet.

The moon, in its feminine aspect, was often said to denote the four faces of woman. The waxing moon represented the face of a young maiden, the full moon was the face of a mother, the waning moon that of a wise grandmother and the dark unseen moon that of the witch or crone. Each indicated the way energies were being reflected in the world.

The dark face of the moon was seen as the potential that was hidden and waiting to come into expression, the waxing moon as that which was developing and coming into maturity, the full moon as the fully developed and mature, and the waning moon as the giving out and sharing of that which has been nurtured and developed. We then return to the dark moon and a period of rest and renewal before the cycle begins again.

THE CYCLE OF THE MOON

The moon takes $29^1/_2$ days to orbit the earth, measured from new moon to new moon. During the course of a complete circuit, the two main impulses are the waxing and waning moon, while the few hours of the full and new moon are characterized by special forces that make its power stronger.

There are four cycles of the moon: the dark or new moon – 4 days (hag), full moon – 3 days (mother), waxing moon – 11 days (maiden), waning moon – 11 days (grandmother).

WAXING MOON

The moon is referred to as waxing in the phase when it first appears as a crescent to when it becomes full. As the moon grows it will exercise a magnetic pull on all things exposed to 'her' energy. It is a time for regenerating, absorbing and creating. It is the perfect time for a fertility ritual, or for psychic protection, or to set off on new avenues of the spirit such as creative projects and business proposals. It is also a good time to plant herbs and flowers.

During the 11 days of the waxing moon everything that you do to build up and strengthen the body is more effective than when the moon is on the wane. The body absorbs more readily, so restorative and strengthening remedies and methods are more effective at this time.

FULL MOON

The full moon is the high tide of psychic powers and can be helpful in all types of ritual and magic. When a special task needs to be completed or a difficult project dealt with, the great power of the full moon is helpful in giving you the energy to complete.

For some people the time of the full moon is a difficult one; they can become edgy and ill at ease, more sensitive and emotional. If you find the power of the moon makes you feel out of balance in any way, avoid performing rituals at this time. Try to understand why the moon affects you so deeply. Use this time to relax and meditate, and learn from these influences about your own powers. It may be that you have been in denial and will become comfortable with yourself and your own rhythms when you begin to examine them. Once you learn to ride the rhythms of the moon you will find that it becomes easier to adjust at this time.

Many people who work in the medical and security professions have told me that during a full moon their business is busier – more people are admitted to hospitals and more people commit crimes. My friend Ali, a midwife, has noticed that more babies are born during the full moon.

WANING MOON

During this period, when the moon goes from full to black, the moon is said to be waning. This is a time for undoing, for receding, for eliminating and separating. If you wish a peaceful ending to a love affair or business partnership, this is the moment to work on it. It is the time to let go of past experiences and undesired parts of your self. In the tradition of witchcraft this was the time to remove warts. In a modern capacity, this is the time to go on a weight-loss programme, to detox, to let go of overindulgence, drinking, drug taking and any other habit. The waning moon is also the ideal time to cut herbs and flowers.

In the past, witches were said to put curses on people during this phase of the moon which were called, appropriately, 'wan-ions'.

THE DARK OR NEW MOON

This is an appropriate time to think over the month, to rest and and evaluate. The new moon is not usually suitable for performing any kind of magic or psychic work. However, some people find that they are more psychic during this phase and may wish to exercise their abilities.

Rituals to honour the power of the moon can be simple or complicated. They range from showing respect to the crescent moon when it reappears to a lengthy ritual celebrating the full moon. I tend to celebrate the new moon just as it begins to wax and show itself as a crescent.

Developing your psychic powers

The Aura

The aura is a personal atmosphere that extends from each person and all living things. When developing psychically, our ability to feel things going on around us is connected with the aura and personal sensitivity. Many of my students ask me questions about the aura such as what is an aura? What does it look like? What is it there for? Basically the aura is like an etheric skin, an extra layer to protect the inner soul and an energetic expression of all our emotions, thoughts and personality. The aura is an energy which is constantly moving, or vibrating, and changing.

The aura is the first sense to pick up the energy of a place. Imagine that the electrical pulses in your etheric body look like very fine hairs similar to the appearance of metal filings being picked up by a magnet; as they stick to the magnet they attach like very fine hairs. The electrical energy around the etheric body looks very similar and it moves and vibrates as it brushes against other frequencies. This is often experienced as hairs standing up on the back of the neck or a cold chill running through the body.

Many people are aware of atmospheres – the good and bad 'feelings' they get from places and people. The human energy field has an atmosphere, a collection of electromagnetic energies surrounding the human body. It appears like an oval-shaped field – not dissimilar to an egg-shaped light prism – which surrounds the body. All living things have an aura and this can be seen or sensed by certain people with a natural sensitivity. Not all psychics can 'see' auras; some 'sense' them. This sensing is an intuitive feeling about the particular energy or atmosphere, colours and textures within the auric field of the person they are being sensitive to.

An obvious way to sense atmosphere is to enter a room or house where there has just been an argument or a death – it feels like walking into a dark cloud. In contrast, the energy in a house where there has been a celebration will be uplifting and vibrant. A home is very much a reflection of a person's personality and an extension of their aura.

The aura, its colours and brightness tell us about the vitality, health and emotions of an individual. All thoughts and memories are contained within this energy field. It is made up of the electromagnetic force of the body, reflecting the physical vitality of a person.

Colours Within the Aura

Our aura is made up of many beautiful rainbow-colour vibrations that form an egg shape around the physical body. The colours of the aura reflect our physical, emotional, mental and spiritual states. When mind, body and spirit are completely balanced and in perfect health, the aura will be a beautiful shimmering rainbow.

As well as giving off our own colour vibrations, we also absorb light energy through our aura. Light is drawn into the auric egg, which acts like a prism, breaking down the light into its component colour elements. The vital energy from light rays, with its seven component colours, provides us with the nourishment that we need to keep us in perfect health. However, if the life force embodied in the seven healing rays becomes blocked then imbalances occur. When this happens certain colour energies build up in some energy centres (chakras) while others become depleted of energy.

Problems in any of these areas show up as bulges or patterns in the shapes of the aura – and energy distortions show up there, too. Eventually, our physical body interprets these energy imbalances as physical illness and manifests a whole array of symptoms in our mental or emotional well-being. Our physical form cannot exist in isolation from our mental, emotional and spiritual bodies; these aspects of our psyche are constantly interacting with one another. Many of our physical feelings are altered by our thoughts and expectations. Building our mental strength and tuning into our intuition influences the colours within our aura, changing negative ones into positive ones.

How to see the aura

Psychic development is often marked by the growing ability to sense or see the aura. I can see the aura vibrating from people's hands and arms then gradually the colour forms on their faces and above their heads. Many people see clear light, but not the colours. Seeing colours often develops later. Sensing the colours of the aura without actually seeing them visually is common.

Seeing the Aura

Find a willing friend and get them to sit or stand still in front of a white background (if you don't have a white wall hang a sheet across the wall). Set up some soft lighting in front of your friend – candlelight is good as it is soft and unintrusive. Sit a few feet away from your friend and put your-selves in a meditative, relaxed or focused state by deep breathing and body relaxation. Now stare steadily at the forehead or third eye of your friend, and allow your physical eyes to lose focus. Remove your glasses if you wear them, and just relax for a few minutes until you begin to 'see'.

The aura first appears as a glow around the head or shoulders, shimmering and moving faintly like soft clouds. It appears as a dim haze, and then brightens. Initially, people tend to see a single colour, depending on the personality of the person you are reading. More colours will appear after a longer watching period and as your confidence grows, you will know what you are looking for. They will appear as coloured clouds, transparent yet quite fixed – even if you blink the colour or light may waver but it does not disappear.

People tend to be able to 'sense' the aura before they can see it. This is through feeling the aura non-visually, by holding your left hand (the more receptive hand) above your head or the head of another person. A tingling sensation will be evident in your hand when it picks up on the auric vibration. Notice where it ends or stops above the crown. Using both palms, stroke your hands along the unseen line of the aura or tingling sensation, running from the top of the head down the body. Do not touch the body physically. The aura stretches out about a foot or more away from the physical body.

The size of the aura is dependent on the person's main activity and also the charisma or power of their personality. Someone who is a mystic or a wise person will have a very light and powerful aura, while someone who is insecure or unwell will have a dimmer and tighter aura. You can sense some-one's emotional state through the condition of their aura. If they are happy-go-lucky they will have a light, positive feel about them, whereas a depressive or angry person will have a much darker feeling about them.

'As a child I always saw people in colour and the days of the week, the season, even certain words. All I had to do was close my eyes and just think about a person and I could feel what they were like. Today I see people's auras and work with colour therapy, so my talent in colour vision as a child has become very useful in my work as a healer.'

Judy, colour healer and Reiki practitioner

As you develop the ability to sense the aura naturally you will begin to be able to see the aura. This should not be confused with two optical effects. The first is when you have been in strong sunlight and see clear dots connected by thin lines floating in front of your eyes. These are not flashes of energy in the atmosphere but cellular debris floating in the eye (a similar sensation occurs when you make a sudden movement from a lying or bending down position). The other optical illusion is the after-image created when you have been staring at something bright for a long time. The flash of a camera, for instance, can leave an after-effect on the eyes.

Seeing Your Own Aura

First focus on your breath and breathe slowly until your body is relaxed. Ambience is important, so use a room with soft or low lighting. It also helps if you are relaxed or tired, so evening is the best time to conduct this technique. When you are physically relaxed your senses are less likely to want to be in control. This enables your intuitive or sensitive side to filter through.

1   Lie in bed or sit down in a chair and hold your hands straight out in front of you. Gaze gently in front of you.

2   Now try fixing your attention on your hands while focusing your eyes on the wall. The hands will appear out of focus but this will help you get a sense of how to look to see the aura.

3   Bring the fingertips of each hand towards each other until they are very close but not touching. The aura should appear as fine lines of light and, if you are lucky, shades of colour – sometimes blue or red. Practise this with just the index fingers.

To increase the auric energy rub the hands together, which opens up the energy flow. The friction enables the aura to expand, making it easier to view. To increase your ability to see the aura, meditate or practise yoga, qi gong or tai chi before beginning this exercise. They help you relax body and mind, and expand your energy flow – which will help to increase perception.

For a few days after you practise seeing the aura, try developing your conscious awareness of the aura in everyday life. Be attentive to your own vibrations and the auras of those around

you – feel, look and tune in to vibrations. Watch how you respond to certain people, places and situations.

Becoming Aware of the Changing Aura

Tune into your own aura and those of others in the following situations. Try this out for a month and make notes of what you observe. Look back at your notes a few months later when you have strengthened your confidence as a psychic and used some of the psychic protection techniques (see section 5, pages 92– 105).

- What is your aura like at different times of the day?
- What are your family's auras like at different times of day?
- Observe the auras of people in your workplace
- What sort of auras do you see in people interacting on public transport?
- Notice how people move in and out of each others auric space, including children, partners, family and colleagues
- Social events – observe what it is about people that attracts you and what makes you pull away from others
- What is your idea of a calm aura?
- What is your idea of an agitated/angry aura?
- When you are calm what colours do you see yourself carrying?
- When you are angry or frustrated what colours do you see inside yourself?

The more advanced student will be able to extend the aura into a place or situation to detect whether they are safe or not within the psychic atmosphere. Try out the following simple technique. Blindfold yourself and go into a friend's house that you are not familiar with. This is to eliminate your physical senses and open you to your intuitive side, which detects through the aura. Go into the main room. As you stand there extend your aura outward from your solar plexus into the space, moving from corner to corner as you feel what you think is in this room. Breathe and relax, then begin to sense the atmosphere or the emotional presence of people who regularly occupy the room. You are sensing without the use of your physical sense of touch or seeing. Hold the vibration of the objects and people inside your aura and interpret what you are picking up. Now share your perceptions of the room with your friend.

All sorts of things affect the aura. Working on a computer, for instance, affects the energy of your aura, as does riding on a cramped train. As people squash against your space their

energy leaves small impressions. If they are feeling positive that will affect you or if they are feeling angry or frustrated this too can transfer into your energy field. However, once you have moved away from the situation this influence almost immediately disappears – unless the interaction was more personal or you are feeling tired or depleted; in these circumstances the negative energy will remain in your aura for a longer period.

Aura Readings and How to Do Them

Once you have practised seeing your aura you may soon start noticing the same effects around other people. The aura encircles the whole body so when you can define colour and intensity of shade, you can begin to read people's auras. For instance if you see a dark shade around someone's stomach region, it may indicate that they could be suffering from a stomach complaint. A similar shade around the head could mean they are depressed or have psychological problems. Bright colours have a more positive diagnosis; they can indicate a happy, healthy disposition and whether someone loves easily or not. Basically, aura reading can diagnose a person's moods, state of health and spiritual energy. In many cases people will have a predominance of one colour while their state of health or mood swings can make the colour change or bring in different colours and shades. You can look up the individual meanings of each colour in the chart that follows, but it is only a rough guide.

When reading someone's aura you can tell them the colour you see and your interpretation of that colour. Once you have the confidence, you can go deeper into your interpretation by using your intuitive skills to give more information about their lifestyle, attitude, state of health and so on. Once you have become an expert at aura readings, you can diagnose a person's mental, emotional and physical energies – even the colours and tones of their astral body (refer to spirit bodies section for more information on the astral body).

When diagnosing someone's aura you need to ask yourself three main questions.

1 What colours do you see?
2 What density is their colour or energy: dark, thick or heavy?
3 If it is light or more transparent is it peaceful or loving, or is there a weakness or loss of energy and therefore an absent sensation?

The main physical areas to focus on are:

• Around the top of the head – this indicates mental state
• Around the third eye – this indicates spiritual state

- Back of the skull – this indicates the state of the subconscious and can help to diagnose any negative areas in the aura
- Around the heart and lung region – this indicates emotional state
- Stomach – indicates the condition of the digestive and solar plexus region
- Base of spine – indicates how grounded and confident in life they are

Main Colours of the Aura

RED

Vitality, strength, power and courage

Red indicates a high level of emotion or stress. It can also be associated with the base emotions of anger, hate, selfishness and lust.

Sometimes red is seen in the aura when someone is convalescing from an illness as a sign that renewed energy and strength is returning to the body. Ambitious and determined people have a strong red tone, generally in the higher part of the aura, as a sign of using their willpower to achieve their ambitions.

PINK

Love, kindness, consideration, selflessness and compassion

This colour indicates a gentle person with high levels of compassion. Pregnant women tend to have pink in their aura.

ORANGE

Happiness, independence, resourcefulness, joy and laughter

This is a powerful colour in relation to healing and cleansing – it has the mix of the power and vitality of red and the positive energy of yellow. If orange is seen around the head or higher parts of the body it suggests someone who is tolerant and open-minded. It is the colour of change and indicates new spiritual aspirations. If the orange is dark turning to a brown hue, it can mean that they are becoming ill or have a tendency to be complacent or depressed. It can also represent an area of the body that is toxic but slowly healing.

YELLOW

Optimism, clarity of thought and knowledge, life giving and self-love

Yellow is the colour of self-expression. It is associated with the solar plexus chakra, a source of pranic energy. If a person has a lot of yellow around their head, it can indicate they have been studying for exams, or using mental activities which are varied and require a lot of concentration. In emotional terms yellow is very positive and optimistic; creative people tend to have a yellow auric dominance.

GREEN

Balance, harmony, nature, self-control, generosity and peace

This is the colour of the heart chakra and many healers have this colour in their aura. A bright green aura suggests someone who is very willing to give and wants only the best for everyone. The stronger the hue of green the more powerful the person. A rich green suggests that they speak only truth, and

they keep their word. Bright green suggests a balanced individual. However, if someone has very dark green in their aura they will probably be very distrustful and dishonest (green with envy).

TURQUOISE
Communication, confidence, strength of concentration and truth
This powerful spiritual colour suggests that the person has a strong, calm nature.

BLUE
Cooling, cleansing, peace, tranquillity, wisdom and the spirit of healing
This highly spiritual colour is the colour of healing. It brings calmness and peace but with a hint of freedom and openness. Many psychics who have the gift of clairaudience have bright blue shades in their auras, as do many creative people such as writers, orators, actors and talkative individuals. If there is a lot of blue in a person's aura it suggests that they are healthy and at peace with themselves.

INDIGO
Intuition, meditation, mysticism and creativity
This spiritual and creative shade suggests someone familiar with the higher chakras, and connected with inspirational energy.

VIOLET
Inspiration, beauty, art, the spirit and high ideals
Violet represents spiritual purity. People who meditate and devote time to their spiritual life have strong purple and violet hews in their aura. It is a royal colour and when a person's soul is highly evolved they will tend to have strong purple shades in their aura, particularly around their head. The darker the colour the deeper their spiritual quest. When a purple shade is mixed with white, the highest shade within the aura, it turns into lavender, which can represent someone who has reached the mountaintop of their spiritual quest.

BLACK
Depression, neurosis and suicidal tendencies
Black clouds in the aura can also represent tiredness, illness and, if the black is more of a grey, it can indicate too much stress and tiredness – even overworking at the office or the body, not seeing enough natural light or nature.

WHITE
Pure pranic energy
White is sometimes seen as flashing lights or pinpoints of bright light in the aura. During healing or meditation, you can see white speckled lights around the head. White signifies health and vitality. It can also mean that spirits and healing energy are present. In psychic circles, white lights indicate the presence of a spirit.

SILVER AND GOLD
Angelic energy
It is unusual to see these colours, as they represent angelic energy. Silver can also indicate quick thinking, mental agility and a fast mind. Gold is a spiritually protective colour and excellent for psychic protection as it represents spiritual strength and power. Kundalini energy (see page 51) is also gold.

Colour Breathing to Influence the Colours of the Aura

Visualization techniques are widely used to aid relaxation and sleep, and in the treatment of cancer and other diseases where available treatments are insufficient. Focusing on a colour can help our concentration and make our thoughts stronger. The colour purple, for instance, seems to have a marked influence on all types of pain. Medical science is beginning to recognize the healing powers of colour visualization, and visualizations are now used extensively to alleviate pain, in times of shock and for stress – in fact, everything from giving birth to the treatment of serious illness. Visualization works because the mind affects the body.

It is possible to influence the colours of the aura using breathing techniques. For instance, you can visualize breathing in white light from a candle flame and on the out-breath breathing out grey smoky fumes which are the emotional and psychic toxins that have built up. Such a technique will lighten the aura.

Colour breathing makes use of the act of breathing together with a focus on colour. It is a powerful method of self-healing and empowers the energy field. By learning how to colour breath you can direct the source of life energy (*chi*) contained in your breath to any part of your body. People who practise colour breathing regularly notice quite dramatic changes in their personal well-being.

To maintain a good level of well-being from colour breathing we need to be able to focus our minds on a particular colour so that a positive blueprint within our thought patterns is picked up through our etheric body into our physical. It is like learning to drive a car; we need to practise consistently before we open up to the process and connect into it automatically. Before embarking on colour breathing it is important to learn how to breathe correctly. Most people do not make good use of their lungs – their breath is shallow and rarely reaches deep into the lungs. Imagine the lungs as two large bags hanging inside your rib cage; every time you breathe they lift and fill up. However, in the majority of cases we don't fill up into the lower part of our lungs, where stale air sits. The deeper we breathe, the more we exercise and the more we open our lungs.

Colour Breathing Exercise

- Make yourself comfortable by lying down on the floor on your back. Feel your spine on the ground and make sure that it is completely straight. Make sure your head, shoulders and arms are relaxed. (If you have any back injuries or weakness, bend your knees and place your feet flat on the floor.)

- Now begin to completely relax your body by tensing and releasing each part. Begin with your toes and then feet, first tensing them up and breathing out when you let go, then work up the body, tensing and releasing each muscle until you reach your head. Roll your head gently from side to side, then open and shut your eyes, relax your jaw, ears and mouth and finally your whole head.

- Now breathe in and out slowly and deeply, surrounding yourself with the colour associated with the area that needs the most attention. For instance, if it is your heart then concentrate on the colour green; if you are in pain use the colour purple. For a general feeling of well-being surround your body with a rainbow, or gold or purple.

WARNING When you have been working psychically or in a development group you will have opened your aura and extended it to pick up energies around the room, so when you complete your work you must bring your aura closer into your body. You can do this by visualizing that you have a cord that you can pull inside your solar plexus to bring the aura closer to your body. Then conduct the normal closing down technique and, if you wish, wrap your energy in a protective cloak (see page 97).

The Power of the Chakras

The aura has seven major focuses of energy, called the chakras. Knowledge about the chakras is a valuable tool for psychic vision, intuition and spirit communication, as well as self-awareness and meditation.

The chakras are psychic centres in the body, they link the physical and etheric bodies and are the doorways into the spirit. They are active at all times, whether we are conscious of them or not. Some healers say that the chakras appear as swirling vortexes of light, or as lotus flowers with varying numbers of petals. The lower chakras are linked with the body and the higher chakras with our spiritual qualities.

The chakras will be explained individually but they function as part of a whole system of energy, rather than functioning independently. Think of the chakra system like a relay race with seven players constantly receiving identical information and responding to that information according to their individual skill.

The three base chakras are represented by the elements of earth, water and fire. They symbolize the concentrations of energy that govern material pleasures. Think wealth, food and sex – all these experiences activate and disturb the three lower chakras. The higher chakras are the heart, the throat, the third eye and the crown. These chakras are connected with our higher aspirations such as love, creativity, truth and the divine spirit. The energy that moves through the higher chakras needs to be purified to enable us to concentrate our inspirational focus in a pure way.

The chakras are the centre of all life. Through the chakras the individual soul is connected to the divine spirit. When we open to Spirit we tune into the ever-present subtle energies that facilitate the soul's journey. Developing body awareness and knowledge is key to opening to psychic powers and the first level is to combine psychic understanding with the spiritual voyage. The journey through the chakras helps us to fully embrace the body, mind and soul.

Indian Yogis have taken chakra energy raising meditations to fantastically high levels – what we are going to look at are very simple methods of engaging and healing the chakras. Before we look at each chakra individually we must first look at the power of the kundalini.

Kundalini Energy

Kundalini energy is the basic energy that drives the chakras. Kundalini comes from the Sanskrit world *Kundal*, which means coil, and kundalini energy is often portrayed as a snake coiled at the base of the spine. It is also sometimes referred to as *Shakti*, which means divine spark or life force. Kundalini is not a term that many understand but it is important to know about this power when working with the chakra system. Yogis believe that kundalini is an aspect of the eternal supreme consciousness. It is through the power of kundalini that all creatures act – it is the power of the supreme will.

The release of kundalini energy is similar to a sensation of waves, flames, pulsations or an uncoiling. The energy seeks an outlet, normally through the spine up to the top of the head and out through the crown chakra into spirit. In the natural evolutionary process, a number of

layers or waves are individually released throughout a lifetime, depending on growth and spiritual readiness (you will see in the section on each individual chakra that the usual ages for this release are given). The movement of this wave is so imperceptible to most people that they are not aware of the activity, though they may be aware of some heat in the tail-bone area prior to the release. Sensitive people will feel the energy progress up the spine, and may feel pressure or pain as the energy encounters a blocked area. This kind of pain is common when we open to psychic and spiritual energy for the first time. The chakras can become stuck like an old door that has not been open for centuries; as the psychic energy moves through the body it opens the door allowing the energy to flood through. Many people feel this sensation during acupuncture, shiatsu and even tantric sex, which are known for their powerful release of kundalini energy!

The power of the kundalini should never be underestimated – it is the divine spark within our body and when it rises it can bring with it periods of heightened awareness and states of bliss or enlightenment. But it is not all positive: as well as highs it can also bring depression, erratic behaviour, mild psychosis, loss of memory and feelings of disorientation with oneself, one's friends and the world in general. This is why many teachers, masters of yoga and various esoteric teachings suggest that an understanding of our own power and will is important in the development of a sound and balanced spiritual energy.

Involuntary Rising of the Kundalini

There are involuntary ways that the kundalini may be released, including drug use, overwork, a severe blow or injury to the tailbone area, and excesses in meditation, tantric sex and yoga. The use of drugs can be especially harmful to your psychic energies, blowing open chakras or causing the 'burnout' experienced by some drug users. Some people use drugs to induce paranormal experiences, to open themselves to higher dimensions and the mystical possibilities in life. However, drug use does not enable a person to achieve this state on his or her own and therefore the energies are not under control, not always very useful – and sometimes exceedingly dangerous.

This book is not about raising the kundalini; it is about raising your awareness to your spiritual and psychic energy. Working with kundalini is best practised with the supervision of an experienced teacher.

The Physical and Spiritual Meanings of the Chakras

The Base Chakra 'Safety and Grounding'

The first chakra is located at the base of the spine between the anus and genitals. It is the foundation chakra – the seat of energy and source of physical strength. Its energy primarily affects the health of your legs, hip joints and base of the spine, as well as your overall physical strength.

One of the main characteristics of the base chakra relates to how well a person can materialize their dreams. Bringing ideas to fruition is directly connected to the process of feeling safe and secure in the world. And we learn about the physical world and how safe we are in it between the ages of 0 and 7, when the base chakra develops. If our needs are satisfied, if we 'lay down roots' for ourselves, then we feel safe to go out and take risks to achieve our aims. This chakra feeds from the energy of the earth.

Common physical problems caused by an imbalanced base chakra include chronic lower back pain, sciatica, varicose veins, rectal difficulties, tumours and cancerous outbreaks located in these areas of the body.

The major psychological issue for the base chakra is a feeling of insecurity in the physical world: a feeling that the world is a threatening place and that you are unable to stand up for yourself or protect yourself; that you don't fit in anywhere, don't belong anywhere and that no place is home; and the fear that comes from not being able to trust that you can materialize your goals. This is compounded by a feeling that you are completely alone in life, and hence feel unsupported and afraid.

If the chakra is balanced then you will feel confident, secure that all your needs will be met and able to ground and centre yourself in any given situation.

COLOUR: red
ELEMENT: earth
SHAPE: 4 petals as a square
ORGAN: anus
GOVERNING PLANET: Mars
ENERGY: male
NEGATIVE ENERGY: fear and darkness

The Second Chakra 'Birth and Death'

The second chakra is located inside the pelvic region. It refines and filters cosmic energy. It has a healing function and links the astral body with the physical. Developed during the years of 8 and 14, which is the beginning of the emotional development of the personality, it governs the element of water and is called the 'dwelling place of the self'. It is the auric gate for astral travel. This chakra controls the vital relationship between emotions and sexuality. It also governs ancient memories of birth and death, the dwelling place of the self where the shadow of spirit resides. Governed by the moon, there is a vital relationship between the water and the moon, and the sacral chakra reflects this by its location, which is close to the womb area in women and the spleen area in men and is very much governed by the emotional tides of life.

The chakra affects the organs of the pelvis, colon and sexual organs. When out of balance it can cause conditions such as menstrual difficulties, infertility, vaginal infections, impotency, pelvic and lower back pain, herpes, slipped discs, all sexual problems, bladder and urinary infections, and cancer of the female organs or prostate.

The major psychological issue for this chakra is power and control in the material world – money, sex and the control of other people. This can manifest as a fear of sexuality, a feeling that you have no power in your sexual relationships, a fear of childbirth, a lack of self-worth, resentment at being manipulated by other people and a sense of being victimized. Participating in any level of dishonesty in your relationships (business or personal) and a fear of never having enough indicates an imbalance in this chakra.

When balanced it gives you a sense of self, and confidence in your sexuality and ability to birth children. You have no problems getting your way with others and are a gifted manipulator.

COLOUR: blue

ELEMENT: water

SHAPE: 6 petals in a circle shape

ORGANS: genitals, womb and its sense organ – the tongue

PLANET: Mercury

ENERGY: feminine, water and lunar (affected by the emotional fluctuations of the cycle of the moon); creativity, sexuality, joy, self-esteem

NEGATIVE ENERGY: fear of sexuality, birth and death; self-deception; sacrifice; nothing excites, nothing pleases and all is lost

The Third Chakra 'Power, Will and Intuition'

The third chakra is located just below the rib cage, where there is a network of nerves called the solar plexus. Known as the emotional mind, this chakra is our psychic battery. It develops between the ages of 15 and 21 – a period when we develop our creativity and confidence within the world. It is the aspect of ego, a sensitive area that responds emotionally to impressions/experiences/people.

The major issue for the third chakra is personal power, fear of intimidation and rejection, and a lack of self-esteem and survival intuition. When this chakra is out of balance it can cause displaced fear and anger to become part of your psyche, and interfere with the development of your fullest capacity as a human being. This can create resentments over having to take responsibility for yourself, personal commitments and finances; a lack of responsibility in looking after another; anger resulting from feelings of neglect or being overlooked; the need to criticize others in order to feel empowered, including taking anger out on safe and helpless victims because of the lack of courage in challenging the source of your own anger.

This is one of the most sensitive chakras. It is where we get our first impression of any person or situation – our gut instinct. The solar plexus is the centre of intuition and provides guidance in daily life.

Physical dysfunctions with this chakra include arthritis, ulcers, all stomach-related complaints, kidney difficulties and liver problems, gall bladder and adrenal gland dysfunctions, anorexia, bulimia, nausea, flu, colon and intestinal problems and cancer of these regions.

COLOUR: yellow/gold
ELEMENT: fire
SHAPE: a triangle surrounded by 10 petals
ORGANS: eyes, digestive organs, feet and legs
PLANET: Sun
ENERGY: male, willpower, creative, immortal, fame, recognition, selfless, charity, ego expression
NEGATIVE ENERGY: need to control, fear of failure, vanity, greed, self-importance, anger

The Fourth Chakra 'Love, Compassion and Balance'

The heart chakra is the highest of the emotional centres and is located in the centre of the chest, just below the sternum. It governs the power of love and has control of the three lower chakras, converting instinct into feeling. It develops during the ages of 22 and 28 years. Compassion, tolerance and sympathy are all emotions governed by the heart.

An out-of-balance heart chakra can cause major issues for the heart including the fear of not being loved or being worthy of love, guilt due to acts of personal rejection or emotional neglect, fear of showing affection, resentment that develops from seeing others receive more love and attention than yourself, emotional emptiness due to experiencing too much loneliness, too much grief and sorrow resulting in a 'broken' heart, and continuing with abusive relationships that are emotionally unfulfilling and damaging.

When this chakra is in balance, you will find it easy to love, to give, to have compassion, to trust your feelings about people and situations, to give without judgment or criticism.

Common physical problems caused by an imbalanced heart chakra include heart attacks, blocked arteries, congestive heart failure, asthma, allergies, lung cancer, pneumonia and circulation problems in the upper back and shoulders.

COLOUR: green
ELEMENT: air
SHAPE: 6 pointed star triangle – pointing upwards as the male principle and downwards as the female principle
ORGAN AND SENSE: hands and touch
PLANET: Venus
ENERGY: life-force, love, peace, calm, feminine balance of male and female, happiness, joy and desire to do holy deeds, learning to give love, share love and receive love
NEGATIVE ENERGY: destruction, abuse, giving too much, martyr tendencies, sacrifice, self-centred, demanding, thoughtless assumption

The Fifth Chakra 'Communication and Creativity'

The fifth chakra is located in the carotid plexus – the throat. It is the first of the three spiritual centres, and develops between the ages of 29 and 35. It expresses its self through communication within the world.

This chakra governs addictions that indicate an inability to command your own power of will and challenge the fears or limitations in your life, i.e. addictions to drugs, alcohol, cigarettes, sugar and food.

The major psychological issues for the fifth chakra involve the development of willpower and personal expression. This manifests as an inability to communicate your feelings – your sorrow, your anger or joy – and your ideas. It can feel as if the heart and throat areas are completely blocked. If you become fearful of self-expression you cannot naturally express your creativity and what is important for you emotionally and physically. You therefore learn to become dishonest with your feelings and deny responsibility for your actions. You direct anger towards yourself and fear the expression of grief, hurt and sorrow. You may allow your own willpower to remain undeveloped and always expect someone else to make decisions for you. You exaggerate or embellish the truth – this includes the habit of gossiping.

When this chakra is in balance you are able to communicate, to be yourself in the company of others, to say what you feel and think, and to be articulate and confident in the way you communicate.

The energy from this centre flows primarily into your thyroid, trachea, oesophagus, neck vertebrae, throat and mouth – including teeth, gums and jaw. Any blockages or illnesses in these areas are therefore due to a dysfunction in the throat chakra. These can include throat and mouth cancers, gum difficulties, teeth problems, stiff neck, laryngitis, tonsillitis, tension headaches, swollen glands and thyroid conditions.

COLOUR: blue
ELEMENT: air
SHAPE: crescent shape surrounded by 16 petals
ORGAN AND SENSE: mouth and hearing
PLANET: Jupiter
ENERGY: knowledge, the power of sound, communication, psychic energy, clairvoyance, calmness, serenity, purity, radiance
NEGATIVE ENERGY: negative intellect, ignorance, using knowledge unwisely, deception

The Sixth Chakra 'Vision and Perception'

The sixth chakra is located between the eyebrows and is referred to as the third eye chakra. In Hindu it is called the *ajna* chakra. The two physical eyes see the past and the present, while the third eye gives insight into the future.

This chakra is the seat of clairvoyance, and links the throat and the crown chakra – the two higher spiritual centres. It develops during the ages of 36 and 42, when self-confidence and discipline allow the development of visions and revelations that go beyond the imagination.

The major psychological issues for the sixth chakra are the use of knowledge, higher reasoning and intuitive skills. Spiritual thinking and spiritual perception are also associated with the sixth chakra. If a 'quality of thinking' has taken root in a person, then it is possible to introduce more advanced thought, which is a process of 'transcendence'. This enables us to rise above day-to-day life and go beyond the self-centredness of the 'me' syndrome. It is the learning of introspection and self-examination. It does not mean that our physical lives – our work, health, families and planet, for example – are not important. It simply enables us to use our mind, both conscious and subconscious, in a rational and clear-sighted way.

Dysfunction in this chakra causes a fear of introspection and intuitive skills; denying the truth, which leads to an inability to discern one's own reality with any degree of clarity; fear that you are inadequate intellectually, and jealous or insecure over creative abilities of another; and paranoid behaviour arising from feelings that you don't know yourself.

The most common physical problems connected to this chakra are brain tumours, brain haemorrhages, blood clots to the brain, neurological disorders, blindness, deafness, spinal difficulties, migraine or tension headaches, anxiety or nervousness – including nervous breakdowns, comas, depression, psychosis, schizophrenia, seizures and other forms of emotional and mental disorders and learning disabilities.

COLOUR: indigo
ELEMENT: all the elements – ether, air, fire, water and earth
SHAPE: circle with two luminescent petals
ORGAN: pineal gland
PLANET: Saturn
ENERGY: authority, command, unlimited power, vision
NEGATIVE ENERGY: self-opinionated, self-delusion, psychosis, misuse of intellectual power

The Crown Chakra 'The Divine Spirit'

The seventh chakra, the crown chakra, is located at the top of the cranium, the cerebral plexus. It represents the Guru within, and develops between the ages of 43 and 49. It is linked with the infinite, the divine source. The crown chakra floods the aura with energy, wisdom, peace and spiritual insights. It is through this centre that the soul leaves the body.

The major psychological issues connected with the seventh chakra are acceptance of one's life, the capacity to fulfil one's purpose and find meaning in life, and the aspiration for a spiritual understanding. This is the place of attitudes, values and ethics. The seventh chakra is the entry point of human life force itself, an invisible current of energy that endlessly pours into the human energy system, nourishing every part of the body, mind and spirit.

Fears and negative behavioural patterns connected to the crown chakra include an absence of faith, a lack of spirituality, a belief that life has no meaning, an inability to see the larger picture at work or in one's life, a fear of self-development (including the fear of knowing oneself), and an absence of courage and faith in oneself.

The organs that are affected by the condition of the seventh chakra are the major body systems such as the nervous system, muscle system, skin and skeletal structure.

COLOUR: white

ELEMENT: ether

SHAPE: a sphere of one thousand lotus petals arranged in the variegated colours of the rainbow

ORGAN: brain

PLANET: Ketu

ENERGY: the guru within, divinity, immortality, reflection of the cosmic self, universal energy

NEGATIVE ENERGY: judgment, orthodoxy, negative intellect, laziness after attaining a state of bliss, misuse of wisdom, manipulation, abuse of spiritual power

As you become familiar with the seven chakras the next phase is to connect with them through meditation. Meditations that involve all seven chakras are extremely powerful in balancing the inner energy of both body and mind, and connecting with the soul. The following meditation is particularly useful for becoming familiar with the location of the chakras in your body and their different sensations.

Guided Chakra Meditation

Take up your usual meditation position. Relax and breathe.

- Begin by bringing your awareness to the root chakra between the anus and genitals. Feel the sensations of the wheel of energy. Breathe into the area and feel the pulsation of the chakra. Let the vibration and the red colour of the chakra radiate out into your aura. Maintain the connection with the chakra for 5 minutes (the more you practise the easier it gets and the more you become accustomed to the energy). Getting to know the energy of your chakras enables you to understand the energy in others.

- Next bring your focus into the second chakra, which is situated about two inches below the navel. If you have trouble visualizing this area, take your right hand and lay it across your belly button with your thumb lying just across the top of it, then use your little finger to press into your belly – there you will find the top of the sacral/second chakra. Feel the sensation and visualize a bright orange light, then let that light shine into your aura. Maintain the connection for 5 minutes.

- Move into the solar plexus, which is just under the rib cage. It is the whole of that region underneath reaching down towards the belly button/navel. Tune into the vibration and visualize the yellow glow of the sun shining inside the third chakra, then let the light out into the aura. Maintain the connection for 5 minutes.

- Now move to the heart chakra, which is located at the physical heart region and that general area. Be aware of its sensation. Visualize a clear green light and then let it spread out into the aura. Maintain the connection for 5 minutes.

- The throat chakra is in the centre of your throat area. Tune into the vibration of the throat chakra. See the brilliant blue light shining inside it, and allow that light to spread out into your aura. Maintain the connection for 5 minutes.

- Next is the third eye chakra, which is located in the middle of and just slightly above your eyebrows. Look into this chakra and feel the sensation. See the colour indigo, watch it glow and then push it out into the aura. Again, maintain the connection for 5 minutes.

- Finally, take your focus to the crown chakra at the top of your head. Feel the golden light vibrate and see the light spread out of the top of your head into your aura, changing into all the colours of the rainbow. Feel the light cascading down through each chakra until it reaches the ground. Maintain the connection for 5 minutes.

When you focus your concentration on the chakras it activates the flow of energy within your body. You can then begin to send this healing energy to parts of your body that are unwell or just tired. When you become confident with this meditation, you can create a flow of light that can embrace your body to bring through your own healing powers, to protect your energy and to help you bounce back when you have been challenged. Meditation and visualization techniques allow us to connect with our inner peace and are a means of connecting with our inner power.

Psychically Awakening the Chakras

The awakening of the chakras happens when you become aware that you are more than just a physical being. The chakras correspond to the spirit bodies and as you become open to a spiritual awareness, either through meditation or practices such as yoga, the chakras become aroused.

Once aroused, there is a tremendous force that moves through your spirit bodies and this begins to open you psychically to the astral level. When the base chakra is awakened you recognize that you are more than a physical being. The second chakra, when aroused, enables you to vaguely remember your dreams (possibly even astral travel) and experience instinctive feelings about people or situations – although you are not sure whether to believe them or not. When the third chakra is awakened you become conscious of all kinds of psychic influences, feeling that some are friendly and helpful, while others are hostile, negative and fearful. This includes feeling that some places are pleasant and others unpleasant, without really knowing why.

When the fourth chakra, the heart, awakens you become aware of the joys and sorrows of others, making you more sympathetic to the physical and emotional pain of others. Arousing the fifth chakra, the throat, can enable you to hear voices, i.e. become clairaudient. You may hear music and sounds both pleasant and unpleasant. The sixth chakra, the third eye, is connected with sight so when it is aroused you become aware of the minute objects, situations with people, see auras and have various sorts of waking visions. When it first becomes awakened you only half-see landscapes and clouds of colour. As you become more adept this arousal brings about clairvoyance. When the seventh chakra is awakened you can feel that you are able to leave your body in full consciousness, and return to it. You begin to feel higher spirits – and communicate with your higher self – and are able to channel information from the spirit world.

A WORD OF CAUTION

There are dangers in arousing the chakras before you are ready. The main problem is that you can become imbalanced psychologically by taking the spiritual journey faster than your mind and body can cope with. It may intensify your perception of the world so that you see the extreme good or the extreme evil in everyone or everything. It could also intensify your psychic skills to the extent that you feel the spirits around you day and night, and this oversensitivity could cause exhaustion and depression.

I recommend that you learn how to meditate on each chakra and bring through a healing power to protect, cleanse and energize them before trying to awaken your psychic connection, as you need to know how to open up and close down (see psychic protection section) before taking further steps in your journey of psychic and spiritual awareness.

Cleansing the Chakras

Chakras are energy transmitting and receiving stations. We transmit energy and we also receive messages from others – sometimes subliminally and at other times in a very aware state. More often than not, the energy of others is an intrusion on our own energy, and may leave us thinking we have moods, thoughts and feelings that are not actually our own. These intruding energies may simply make us feel heavy and tired, or they can also be serious enough to cause pain or make us think we have an illness.

Exercise is very important in helping to even out the energy from our own patterns, as well as those we pick up from others. Many of these energetic conditions work themselves away from our body – particularly if we engage in physical exercise such as going to the gym, running, aerobics or any other cardiovascular forms of exercise. I find that because I give too much from my heart chakra, I get congested in my heart and lungs, so working out in they gym and releasing tension from my chest helps.

Yoga, tai chi and qi gong are also excellent for keeping the etheric body and the nervous system clean and vibrant. Dancing is also a super way of releasing tension – particularly emotional and sexual tension. The alternative to all this exercise is rest. Rest can make all the difference to your energy levels. I find lying outstretched in the garden with my spine directly on the ground for half an hour gives me more energy than sitting in front of the television for two hours. Alternatively, try a yoga position called the child's pose – spending 15 minutes in this pose can give you more energy than sleeping for an hour.

Healing the Chakras

The word heal comes from the word 'whole', suggesting that in order to heal we must treat the whole being – body, mind and soul. Modern medicine tends to concentrate on the body at the expense of the mind and soul – but this is changing. More and more people are beginning to realize that our physical health is inexorably connected to our emotional and spiritual health.

The chakra energy system is a natural organizer of human stress, in that each chakra centre responds to specific human life issues. In learning about the life issues that are associated with each chakra, one can begin to understand which stresses are likely to disrupt specific areas of the body – because every stress is connected to a psychological reaction. For instance, stress that accompanies fear of failure will directly affect the stomach, upper intestine, pancreas, liver or spleen because fear of failure directly relates to the issues of the third chakra.

Healing the Chakras with Crystals

The healing power of crystals is widely recognized. Crystals can absorb and store power, and we can release this power by consciously directing our energies through them. Healing the chakras with crystals is an essential part of self-healing and invaluable for healing others.

It is best to attempt crystal healing on others before you attempt self-healing. If you initially practise on yourself you become too familiar with your own energy and will then fail to understand energy blocks and psychic disturbances when you begin working on other people.

You can use any of the following crystals for healing: clear quartz, rose quartz, smoky quartz, amethyst or citrine. For healing I find clear quartz works best. It is the easiest to use and the most willing to be a receptor of healing power. When healing with crystals it is important that the tip is not cracked or blemished. The crystal should be natural and not polished or artificially manufactured. Crystals, semi-precious stones and precious stones may be damaged in the mining process, this condition will remain in the stone affecting the user, therefore it is wise to clear the crystal first before use (see page 116).

Some healers place various types of crystals on the body at the points of the chakras and aura to ground, cleanse and purify the energy system. The technique which I find most helpful is using the crystals within a pendulum.

Healing the Chakras with a Crystal Pendulum

Before attempting this technique you must have a good knowledge of the chakras – where they are within the body, their colours and meanings. It is important if you do this type of healing and diagnosis of emotional and spiritual conditions, that firstly, you are aware of the power of the crystal you are using and secondly, make sure if you work on a friend that you are fully aware of the subtle power of working with people's energy. Not only could you cause disturbance in the person you are working with, but it may also have an effect on you. I have had clients call me who have practised this technique on their partners and have found that they have taken on some of their energy. So only work on a friend or partner if you have a thorough understanding of chakras and the crystals. And ensure that you ground yourself before and after the healing session (see page 95).

Crystal Healing

Chakra diagnosis is conducted with a crystal pendulum. It should show how the chakras are energetically charged. You can discover the flow of energy through the body, and note how the chakras are functioning – whether they are healthy, filled with vitality, low on energy or blocked. You can set up a chart of questions to ask the pendulum before you begin.

Create the 'right' atmosphere in the room – light a candle, burn incense or smudge the room with a herb stick (see making a sacred space section). Ask the power of the divine/universal energy/God to bless the healing. Link in the way you feel safe or try as many methods of linking in until you find the one that suits your nature. There is no 'right' way, while one person may put on an elaborate act to prepare, another person will simply recite a prayer to ask for a blessing.

1 Begin by getting the person to lie on the ground – either on a blanket or just on the floor. They need to be comfortable so you can place a cushion under their head, and have their knees raised up if their lower back has any tension or discomfort. Instruct them to close their eyes, and align their neck, head and spine. Now instruct them to breathe deeply through their nose and out of their mouth to release any tension in the body. Repeat the breathing three times.

2 Once you feel that they are relaxed, hold the pendulum in your right hand, which is your power hand, and hold it with your thumb and forefinger. Let the crystal dangle loosely so it has the freedom to move in whatever direction it chooses to without any physical pressure from you.

3 To receive the vibrations of the chakra, hold the pendulum about two inches above the chakra and watch which way it turns, whether it traces a circle, or an ellipse or if it swings in straight lines. Repeat the procedure for all seven chakras. It is important to remember the way the

pendulum moved around each chakra in turn, and make a note of what you perceive as the behaviour of the crystal. For instance, if the first three chakras are out of balance you will find that the heart chakra, which is the centre point of the body, will be affected by the lower three and therefore the energy reaching into the higher three will also be either too busy or not active enough.

4 To diagnose each chakra, hold the pendulum over the chakra at the centre of its energy source and watch the way the pendulum moves. If it moves anticlockwise it has activity which may be negative, such as anxiety or fear. If it stays still it generally means that there is a block, which could be unconscious – suggesting that they have either forgotten about a situation which affected them during that particular development in their life or that they are very peaceful with themselves in that chakra and what it represents energetically. If it moves clockwise and steadily it is a healthy chakra and is not blocked. If it moves in an agitated fashion it may represent current issues that are troubling the person, issues connected with the energy of that chakra.

5 Once you have diagnosed each chakra, you then cleanse the crystal with incense, a smudge stick or place it in salt water.

6 Next, to help release blocked energy, begin working on each chakra, starting with the base chakra and moving upwards. Hold the tip of the pendulum about two inches above and draw small circles with the crystal pendulum. Draw seven circles on each chakra, which is enough to bring up the energy that may be blocked, and not too much so you can cause disturbance with the energy within the chakra. Pull the crystal upwards and away from the chakra when you finish.

7 Having worked on each chakra you now return to working on the base chakra, again making seven small circles and drawing the pendulum away when it feels heavy on your arm, this generally means that you have released an energy block. Do the same with each chakra

8 To test whether the healing is working return to each chakra, hold the pendulum over it – if it swings naturally over the chakra in a clockwise direction then you have cleared it.

9 If you find difficulties with one or more chakras when you have completed the whole system, return to the ones that showed signs of remaining blocked. The crystal is like a magnet drawing up anything that it has connected to; sometimes it takes a little longer when the wounds are very deep. If the chakra remains blocked there are issues still surrounding the person in connection with that particular chakra. It is recommended that these issues are addressed before you work on them again.

I have found that chakra healing with crystals creates an immediate response in clients, but only on a delicate level at first. If someone is naturally sensitive they will notice the difference but if you are working on someone who is insensitive they may say that they don't feel any different or that they are simply more relaxed. The most physical reaction is experienced in the third chakra as this governs the digestive organs and the majority of people in the West hold a lot of anxiety in the solar plexus.

This type of healing is not designed to cure people of serious physical and mental conditions but to balance the energy levels and alleviate tension, thus bringing about a state of calmness and well-being. It is generally recommended that you have this treatment once a week to help release work tension and day-to-day stresses. Its the psychic equivalent of going to the gym for a bodily pick me up. For deeper healing of the chakras, go to a professional healer or health care practitioner.

The Spirit Bodies

The subject of spirit bodies may be a little esoteric for many students of psychic development but it is essential to have an understanding of the mechanics of the spirit realms and how we are connected to our spirit. I will only briefly cover each of the spirit bodies but once you have familiarized yourself with the aura and the chakra system you should seek out some in-depth books on this subject. Many have been translated from the Indian Vedic teachings by the Theosophical society and other occult and psychic societies (see Resources, page 180).

The soul is the bridge between body and spirit, heaven and earth; only in this function does it have meaning in life. If we can see the soul as a bridgehead between the material world and the spiritual realms we can then bring the two worlds together to work in harmony. To be able to do this we need to understand the many levels that function within us as a human being and as a spirit. The physical body is a complex affair and the many layers of spirit bodies that act as shells or covers to the soul are no less intricate.

The human form can be viewed as having five major spiritual parts.

The Physical – the body
The Etheric – energy
The Astral – emotional or psychic
The Ego – mental
The Spiritual (causal) body – divine

Each spirit body has its own function and each needs to operate singly, or with the others, with guidance from a divine level. Our life force flows better when there is harmony among the spirit bodies.

The densest of bodies, and the only one readily seen, is the physical. The other bodies vibrate at higher levels. There are actually seven spirit bodies that make up who we are as a whole, but the four main levels which we function on are the physical, emotional, mental and spiritual. Most people interact with others and the world only through a few of their spirit bodies. A person may be primarily 'physical and emotional' or 'physical and mental', or perhaps 'mental and spiritual'. This means that they work through those aspects of themselves more than others. Someone may be very emotional or overintellectual, therefore they function more in either their emotional body or their mental body.

The Physical Body

To be effectual in psychic work, you must be fully 'in' your physical body and feel your body is firmly connected to the earth, or grounded.

How much are you in your body? How do you feel about yourself and being in your own body? It is important to be aware of how well grounded you are as this indicates whether you need to work on bringing your attention into the physical or if you are too physical and need a little more aesthetic or spiritual influence in your life.

HOW WELL GROUNDED ARE YOU?

This question is asked frequently in new age and stress management workshops. But how many people really understand it? To be grounded is to know the earth; to recognize instinctively how to deal with any situation or with any type of person. When you have interacted with a grounded, instinctive person you will feel safe and cared for, while someone who is ungrounded will leave you feeling unconnected. One of the keys to knowing whether you are grounded is by the way you breathe. Can you breathe in and out in a tranquil and controlled manner? If you can then you will find that you are comfortable about being in your body: if not then you may have emotional and psychological issues that need to be addressed.

People are often ungrounded because of a difficult childhood, trauma, illness, etc. But there are methods that can be used to enable people to reconnect and become grounded and happy with themselves. This takes time and a great deal of healing with professional therapists,

but once the pain has been sourced and a healing programme applied then a grounded connection with one's self naturally happens.

Make a checklist of what threatens you; what stops you feeling grounded and safe in all situations. If threatening situations – be they simple criticism or some form of physical threat – send your consciousness into a state of panic, disturbance, irritation, loss of control and so on, then your body will experience anxiety. This triggers a flow of adrenalin and the classic fight or flight stress response. If on the other hand you can find a quiet space inside, your body will trust you enough to deal with the challenge. This is more than self control, it is empowerment and confidence.

Once you have acknowledged the importance of being in your physical body, you can then move on to find out how much you are aware of your higher spiritual energy. It is essential that you learn to become comfortable with your physical body and ensure that you take care of your health and mental well-being before pursuing higher spiritual practices.

The Etheric

The first level beyond the physical is the Etheric. The Theosophists were the first to describe the etheric body in detail to the Western world. Its philosophy stems from the East and teachings such as Hinduism and Buddhism, but psychically gifted people throughout all ages and cultures have been aware of the Etheric.

The etheric body vibrates around the physical body like an extra skin and plays an important part in our psychic ability to sense things intuitively. It extends a few inches away from the physical body as the etheric aura, and within it are the many energies and forms containing the chakras, as well as acupuncture meridians and life-giving *chi*. The etheric body is the envelope or sheath made of *chi*. The Etheric permeates the entire physical body just as *chi* does. It does not sit inside the physical body like the ego or the soul but is a part of the life force of the body. The Etheric extends beyond the physical. For instance, in Tibetan medicine the traditional doctors may perform acupuncture on certain energy points situated beyond the limits of the body, moving the energy within the Etheric.

As long as you are alive, the physical and etheric bodies remain closely associated. The Etheric is the emanation of the physical and the body cannot survive without it. An example of sensing the Etheric is when someone who has had limb amputated can still feel it even though it is no longer physically there.

It is from this energy matrix that *chi,* or life force, is distributed to the physical body. The etheric body also acts as a transmitter and receiver of emotional and mental thoughts, patterns, ideas and energies from the higher spiritual levels and the physical energies from below. There is now evidence of the form of the aura with its colour and texture through Kirlian photography. There are psychics who see the aura as an interplay of colours, but very few are able to see deeper and higher energy levels such as the chakras or the flow of physical energy or *chi.*

The Astral Body

The astral body can be defined as the layer in which thoughts and emotions are contained. It is also referred to as the desire body as it reflects our true desires. It is the place where we use our intuition or gut instincts. The astral body is like an emanation that extends some distance outside of our body – a little like antennae. For instance, when we meet someone for the first time, or find ourselves in a strange place, the astral body picks up and transmits sensations to us about the energy of the person or place. The astral body makes us sensitized. It is our emotional body and it senses things about people and places before we are able to confirm what we know about them logically. For instance when two people are attracted, the two energy fields blend by extending towards each other. Conversely, anger and strong feelings of dislike create barriers between these energy fields.

The astral body is in a constant state of flux and movement as it mirrors all changes of emotion and responds to the moods and vibrations of others. For instance, you can become depressed simply by entering a room where there is someone who is depressed or when the room itself has a low atmospheric energy. This is the astral body responding to exterior emotions. In the same way, a healer may absorb the symptoms they are working to heal. Someone who is clairsentient has a 'feeling', a 'knowing', a 'smell' and follows it – they are sensitive to situations and to moods of people that are close to them. Oversensitivity to others can be a problem and those who find it traumatic need to learn how to protect themselves when in a crowd, doing healing work or when sympathizing with another person's problems (see psychic protection section).

Working with your Astral Body

The astral is connected with the thoughts, emotions and reactions of our ego. As a healer I can feel the astral body when working on the physical body. It vibrates and moves with a fluidity – particularly with people who are healthy, and even more so with people who meditate

and cleanse their psychic energy. If a person has been drinking alcohol or taking drugs or been very ill, their energy flow is denser and less fluid, particularly in the parts of their body which appear to be stressed or ill.

You can feel this for yourself if you place yourself into a state of meditation or become quiet. Initially you do not connect with your spirit or a divine energy, but experience the sensation of the constant movement – the ebb and flow – of the astral body. The astral can be so dense in some people that it blocks off the connection with the higher self. It is important, therefore, that you keep your energy clean and look after your physical body – so you can become spiritually aware and connect with a spiritual intelligence. As you become more aware of your spiritual side you will be bombarded by many messages from the psychic realms, the spirit world and even your own soul. To keep this channel clear the astral has to be maintained in working order. So as well as keeping yourself fit, physically and emotionally, keep your chakras clear. The chakras have an influence on the state of the astral body and chakra clearing exercises (see pages 60–65) keep the energy balanced.

Astral Travelling

Astral travel is associated with the astral body. It is the power to leave the physical body and 'fly' to other places. Mystics in India are trained to place their bodies in a death-like state for three days, during which time they travel into the spirit worlds. Once their journey is complete they are called back to their bodies. Examples of astral travel have also been recorded by people who have had near-death experiences. However, it is not necessary to be in a death-like state to astral travel – it is possible to do the same without any danger to our health.

The chakra associated with the astral body is the second chakra, this is located in women between the ovaries and in men at the spleen centre, the physical location is about two inches below the navel, it is a place of clear feeling, as well as astral travel.

I have only once felt the physical sensation of astral travel but I've experienced it in lucid dreams when I knew had been to visit people or places. The difference between dreaming and astral travelling is that the feelings and colours within the astral journey dream were brighter and certainly more physical than normal dreams.

Astral Travel Technique

- Lie in bed and place your body in a deep state of relaxation. Systematically release tension from each muscle, beginning at your toes, moving through your legs and pelvis into your chest and shoulders, arms and hands until you reach your face and head. Now move down through each vertebrae in the spinal column, back down the legs to your feet. You should now feel relaxed and as if you are floating (this may take a little practice). The purpose is to detach your mind and body from each other.

- Now let your breathing become slow and deep. Focus your attention on the centre of your forehead, your third eye, as you settle into rhythmic breathing.

- As you begin to let go notice how heavy your body is feeling, and that your spirit bodies are light and weightless. Set your attention on your astral body – imagine that you are connecting with it. Ask that the divine being that guides and protects you remain with you as you journey. Now see the astral as a body of light, just like your physical body but lighter: picture in your mind's eye images of sunlight, feathers floating on the breeze. This releases your astral being from your physical.

- At this point some people begin to see psychically even though their eyes are closed. Things appear bathed in a purple light. If you get this far focus your attention on the ceiling light fitting so you can start to travel outside of the body.

- Imagine drawing the light bulb towards you. As you do this you will feel yourself floating upward towards the ceiling. Try to do this consciously. You will become aware of floating in your astral body and if you are lucky you may even see your physical body lying below you on the bed.

- As you begin to move through in to the astral realm ask your guide to return you safely to your body when you have completed your journey.

- When you want to return to your body, just think of returning and you will return gently. Getting back into the body is easy, getting the technique right to get out is much more difficult!

The Mental Body

The mental body is composed of two aura bands, known as the higher and lower mental bodies. The lower mental body is the rational, conscious mind, the place of reality. It is also known as the place of thought forms and the seat of the desire mind. It is significant in all psychic work, particularly in visualization and manifestation of psychic energy and spirit contact. The higher mental body is the inspirational, the imagination and super-conscious level of the mind, the place of limitlessness and creative consciousness. The two bodies are intricately linked as most people cannot discern their higher self from their thoughts.

The lower mental body is associated with the solar plexus chakra. The higher mental body is connected with the heart, the place of empathy and compassion, of oneness with others and non-rational thinking, imagination and intuition.

The higher the level the faster the vibration: for instance the Etheric vibrates more rapidly than physical dense matter, the emotional body vibrates more rapidly than the Etheric and the mental body, with its thought forms, vibrates more rapidly than the astral body. Therefore it is believed that fewer psychics see thought forms visually than see the emotional aura, and fewer see the astral body than see the Etheric.

Thought Forms

Thought forms are created in the mind, but not the 'physical' brain, and transmitted by way of energy that is the 'spaces between atoms' or *chi*. Psychics see them as whirling objects in the emotional aura.

Psychokinesis is the power of mind over matter using thought forms to create psychic phenomena. Psychokinesis occurs in bursts of energy in the shape of thought forms. These thought forms create physical concrete world changes by transmitting energy or life force through the psychic bodies. A mental idea moves through the mental level to the emotional body, then makes changes in the Etheric before changes in the physical happen. Ideas and thought forms originating from the spiritual bodies move from the spiritual down into the mental levels and so on. Thought progression can also move from the physical into the psychic realms.

To achieve a physical phenomena through thought requires willpower and great focus. Examples are in laying on of hands during spiritual healing or direct transmission of energy through physical activities such as tai chi and qi gong where you are moving and opening the energy flow from the physical into the spiritual and back into the physical.

Telepathy on the other hand is the transmission of thought forms directly to the mind of another. This occurs in clairvoyance from the spirit realms and in absent healing. This energy is controlled and concentrated by the mind. With thought forms you can create changes in the aura and transmit auric energy, for instance when you expand the aura, energize the aura and open and close down.

Sarah Higbid, a UK-based costume designer, has found that since opening up to psychic work she sees purple floating clouds of light before she goes to sleep. She says it gives her a very comforting feeling – a cloud on which she drifts peacefully into the dreamtime.

Opening The Third Eye

In opening the third eye we begin to develop more towards psychic seeing in picture forms and symbols, either within our mind's eye or in a physical form. Here we are using our mind's eye to make the transition from meditation to psychic vision. Practise this exercise on a daily basis.

• Focus on a candle flame or object to take the physical eyes to a point, then focus on the third eye just above the eyebrows. Now ask your mind to concentrate on the psychic levels. In the beginning you will probably see energy – floating energy forms that may just be soft hues of light without colour, though some may see colour. The colour becomes more intense the more you practise. When you begin to see shapes and forms you are seeing into the etheric level – some people see as it a fuzzy energy in the atmosphere. This is the ether.

The more advanced student may see lights and shades around trees or plants, rooms and even people; while adepts can see spirits of the dead looking just as they once did on earth. Later you may find that you can see into the spirit world, and astral levels.

The Mind – Connecting to the Spirit

It is important to perceive the function of the mind and how it influences our psychic connection. To understand your psyche, begin by breaking down the influences on your mind into several layers. Start with the ego consciousness, which is the identity of your human personality – the person you have become due to the influences of family and environment. The other aspects, which are the unconscious, resonate their influences into our personality

from a subtle and yet powerful arena of our many subpersonalities, which have developed from our memories of childhood, and from our family and ancestral influences.

Finally there are the influences from our spirit – these are termed higher consciousness. These aspects have an important bearing on our overall capacity to connect with spiritual and psychic powers and are the reason some people have a natural connection while others do not. If you allow yourself the time to work out each influence and see your character formed from these aspects you will begin to acknowledge how your mind functions. (This is a vast and complicated arena to delve into. If you are drawn to the understanding of your mind then you should study character analysis and psychology – especially the teachings of Carl Jung, whose interpretation of the mind allows a spiritual as well a scientific means of understanding human consciousness.)

Assessment of the Mind

1 **YOUR PERSONAL IDENTITY**   Identify who you think you are and what you perceive yourself to be. Many of us believe that the time and the place of our birth, the pattern at that moment in the heavens, the shape of our body, our hands, our head … are part of the basic blueprint that we have to work with in life. As we discover ourselves through different experiences in life, we uncover our physical, emotional, mental and spiritual characteristics and the fact that they are all entwined. You can begin by identifying yourself by your physical body type: how you perceive your physical characteristics such as your physical strength, your beauty, your ability to maintain a healthy body, etc. Next look at your emotional identity. How do you express yourself at any given moment? Inside our emotions there is the child, the adolescent and the adult. Try to assess your own character, form a description to identify how you perceive yourself at each stage of development – when you are being the child, when you are functioning as the teenager, when the adult is working in your life. Think about how these aspects of your personality affect your behaviour.

With mental and spiritual identities begin by building up your characteristics through the various forms of assessments such as astrological studies, palmistry, through Chinese medicine or Ayurvedic medical analysis.

2 **THE UNCONSCIOUS**   These are aspects of your ancestral line that influence your mind, body and spirit. The traditional system of race and ancestry is widely recognized, and the perception of racial differences and family tradition still play a powerful role in an individual's sense of identity.

Go back into your family history (as far back as you can go) and plot your family tree with the help of your living family and a genealogist. If you find this process too difficult, then you can use meditation techniques to visualize your family and their influence in your life today. Your ancestry affects the way you perceive yourself to be within the world: how you feel emotionally and how you are physically. This includes any genetic illnesses and conditions that may be passed through the family tree, as well as any mental problems and psychological characteristics.

3 **MIDDLE UNCONSCIOUS**   This aspect of the mind is connected with the development or evolution of your personality. This is influenced by the cerebral cortex, the part of the brain which has gifted us with consciousness and the ability to say 'I think therefore I am'. This part of your personality can be assessed through psychometric testing, which is designed by psychologists to provide a clear analysis of your thinking personality.

4 **FIELD OF CONSCIOUSNESS**   This is how you tune into your psychic powers. It becomes developed through working with your psychic powers, and is your conscious connection with the unseen. It touches our physical life, for instance, when we sense atmospheres or communicate telepathically with another person, or if we are clairvoyant, clairsentient or clairaudient.

5 **SUPER CONSCIOUS**   This is our connection with the universe and all of life. It is the divine aspect of our mind which connects with us – in the majority of cases in an unconscious way. We are not aware of this connection unless we are provoked by extreme emotions, or a powerful spiritual experience that touches us so deeply for that moment we can feel God in all of life.

6 **COLLECTIVE UNCONSCIOUS**   This is our connection with all living things on this planet since the beginning of time.

The Intuitive Mind

One of the most startling implications of present research on the nature of our brain is the discovery that the two hemispheres of the brain function as separate spheres of consciousness, each with its own agenda and personality. There is a belief that an intuitive person has greater access to both hemispheres.

Many intuitives and psychics have difficulty in distinguishing between what is real and what is visionary, and what is internally or externally generated. When this is coupled with a lack of

confidence to act on what is intuitively felt, then an understanding of the mechanics of visionary experience is essential.

There are certain areas of the brain which, when stimulated, will produce intensely real and inspired visions. One area of the emotional system – sometimes called 'The God Spot' – triggers a euphoric feeling of being in a divine presence. This occurs because the auditory cortex and speech areas can yield inner voices that are most likely a feedback of your own thoughts. However, such pragmatic explanations do not account for the sheer diversity of experience that the intuitive mind channels. For people with these unique talents, psychic phenomena can come in various guises – sound, sight, smell, touch and taste.

The main weakness for intuitive types is that the emotional charge behind the imaginative vision makes it almost impossible for them to distinguish what is real and what is imagination. It is a difficulty experienced by all those who are psychically gifted and the reason why proper training is important if you are to gain accurate and precise information from your psychic impressions. To maintain a connection with a clarity of vision it is recommended that you learn to meditate and contemplate your inner vision and feelings, and continue to listen and see what life brings to you – as lessons, as inspiration and as experiences. Life is for living and only by living can we develop a true vision of life.

The Causal Body

The causal body is the first of the spiritual bodies. It serves as a balance between the personality and the other spiritual bodies. It is also a vehicle for contact with the universal mind that brings insights and understandings to our human level. It is believed that as a soul comes down through the various levels from the causal, through the astral and physical realms it takes on the coverings, or bodies, in order to be able to communicate and exist at those levels.

The soul, when it reaches into the higher mental state, is shrouded as it integrates with the causal body. The cloak of the causal covering is so subtle that even the mystics or spiritual masters believe that they have reached the final source, the regions of light where the inner being of the souls of these regions are steeped in deep bliss, love and peace.

The causal field is grounded in spiritual reality; it interpenetrates the individual's mental field and also connects with the universal energy. As human experience is invariably dualized into me and not me, this energy serves as a bridge between levels of unity and duality. In the classic mystical experience there is an overwhelming sense of oneness – the distinction between me and not me simply does not exist.

This only happens to someone who has little awareness of this level when they touch on a mystical moment called the body of bliss. This is the place of intuition and compassion. During development of a connection with this higher level that pure intuition and wisdom can come from this aspect of ourselves. It may not always be accurate and focused – unless grounded through the other bodies such as the mental and astral – as the inspiration will have no physical reality and will appear too dreamy and unrealistic. But it is worthwhile being patient and working on a spiritual intelligence through meditation, going on spiritual retreats and working with spiritual masters and gurus who can offer us mere mortals an understanding of the divine incarnate. In time we may learn to bring an aspect of the divine into our daily life.

Understanding our divine purpose is the highest spiritual principle. To achieve the blissful sensation that occurs when the physical body has been encouraged by spiritual disciplines to be transformed into a divine reflection of God – to understand divine power as a frequency or vibration – requires soul searching within our destiny. When this point is reached inner peace is found and our soul can become part of our body, and mind.

The relationship between the physical and subtle energies is complex. The subtle level of our being indicates hidden levels of potential within us all. Being conscious of our true nature is a difficult and often painful process. It requires commitment, freely given, to follow the path towards our own enlightenment. It necessitates working with consciousness and with our own depths. The process requires that we slough off old levels of identification as many times as is necessary. This is the ageless quest for the ultimate reality; it takes many forms and is at the heart of all true spirituality.

The Spirit/Divine Body

Our relationship to the Divine is beyond words and theory – often this is where we find spiritual renewal. We have been taught for thousands of years that our bodies are unclean, that we were not made in the image of the Divine, and that we must split spirituality from matter. Of course, in doing so, the intuitive and creative have been exiled, and a barren trap of self-doubt, self-hatred and a separation from the Divine has been erected around many of us.

By reuniting our bodies with our spirit, we can move out of the often deadening rational place of trying to have a relationship to the Divine. We can then move into a holy or sacred knowing that we are Divine, that we are part of the whole. A body-based relationship to spiritual renewal can also get us past our fears of being intimate with the Divine by helping us honour our bodies and acknowledge the Divine within us: the similarities between our bodies and the earth and between our regenerative powers and the regenerative power of life. In the end, the spiritual life is not one of intellect; it is knowing in the physical body that we are all one.

Tuning into Your Spirit Bodies

BRING IN THE LIGHT
Lie down and relax in your sacred space and bring about a feeling that you are floating.

- Ask to be aware of your divine spirit body. Ask it to be filled with God's presence. Let the energy come into the causal body and proceed down to each of the bodies, ending with the physical. Spend a few minutes of reflection at each level before you move into the next level.

- Note the sensations and images that you may receive as you move through each spirit body.

BRING IN THE BALANCE
Next you are seeking to bring harmony to aspects that are out of balance, for instance where there is too much power and focus in one area or too little in another.

- Begin with the physical body, and ask to be in touch with each spirit body in turn. Ask each body its opinion on which level has too much control or input and the aspects which may not have enough. Ask each body how it feels about its role within the seven aspects of your spiritual being.

- If you can manage to sense a response, note as many changes as you feel would be appropriate to make. However strange the images that you may receive are – whether they are colours, or textures or just feelings – trust what you sense and make the decision that you will make changes in your life to rebalance those energies.

Communication with spirits

*T*alking to spirits is part of the development of psychic awareness. While some of us may communicate with spirits very easily, others need to spend time learning how not to be too afraid and how to communicate with the spirit world in a confident and safe way.

Spirits appear as presences or paranormal manifestations – as on-going companions seen or unseen – in dreams, meditations or at quiet times. There are several types of spirit companions or guides; some that come and go, and others – the lifetime guides that are with us from childhood – that are permanent. Spirit beings are as interested in us as we are in them. We are fascinated by them because of our need to be supported and loved, while they are interested in our physical world and us as individuals because they need to be heard and still maintain a relationship with the living. They can assist us to recognize and embrace our creativity, attract success and to find our spiritual qualities. Spirit guides are there for everyone and throughout the ages we have called them a variety of names from gods and goddesses of nature to guardian angels and ancestral spirits.

Spirit Guides

The notion of a spirit guide is a very old one – think, for instance, of the 'guardian angel' of the Catholic faith. A spirit guide is an entity who accompanies you throughout your life, looking after you and your spiritual development.

A guide is a generic term for helpful spirit, a spirit who assists people throughout their life-time. They are different to a relative or ancestor; they primarily look after your spiritual development and represent your connection with God/Divine. They relate to our past-life memories and believe that they have a connection with us from a particular past life. They are caring and have a compassionate attitude towards the planet and humanity. They are aware of your 'book of life' – your destiny – and will encourage you to make the right decisions to encourage your personal growth.

Recently a client came to see me for healing. During the session I felt the presence of a Native American spirit who I felt was her guide and who had been with her since childhood. He spoke to her about how when she was very young she used to have pains in her legs that the doctors couldn't diagnose. He said that she was his daughter in a previous life where she had had a terrible accident and lost the use of her legs. This memory touched her deeply and she told me after her session that she had always believed that she had lived before and had had a passion for Native American culture for as long as she remembered. It comforted her to know that there was a guide who loved and cared for her.

Types of Guiding Spirits

Relative

This is a person who you would have known and, now deceased, wishes to help you from the spirit world. They communicate through you with an intuitive guiding voice and many have their own opinions on how you should conduct your life. In some cases it may be helpful, in others it is best to give their opinions the same amount of consideration you would have when they were alive. In general these souls only have good intentions. In many cases they are with you only while you are going through a tough patch.

Ancestor

These spirits are family members who you will not have met – they exist in the spirit world and guide living descendents. In some families there are conflicts within the ancestral line while in others there is a supportive network of spirits. There can be some very wise and caring spirits who are tireless in their work for the evolution of the family tree and come when there is a birth or death within the family.

Occasionally ancestors have found it difficult to let go of the family and can cause physical and emotional distress to their descendents. In China and the Far East ancestral prayers are conducted on an annual basis to ensure that any renegade or negative ancestral members are unable to influence the living.

Guide

Guides are to do with spirit communication. Some guides are backed up by their own team or network of spirits. This is usually overseen by a higher guide, who will from time to time work on a direct level with a channel or medium, using them to offer their wisdom and compassion.

Guides and guardians tend to be old souls with wonderful vibrations. You can sense them when they channel through a medium or when they enter a room during meditation or prayers – they can impose an immense feeling of safety and peace. I believe that they connect with your soul from past life memories – a possible reason why so many guides are from ancient countries and cultures such as Africa, Asia, India, Tibet and China, as well as Native Americans of North and South America and Aborigines from Australia.

My husband, Terry, had a 7ft African guide (his doorkeeper) called Chumba when I first met him. When he walked into the room you could feel this peaceful yet awesome presence. He was a wonderful ally for Terry when he began his work as a soul rescuer in his early twenties.

Guardian Angels

Angelic spirits are the guardian spirits who protect and guide families, tribes and communities. The majority of people communicate with them through prayer or meditation. When you open up to higher levels of frequency or energy, you can connect with these angelic beings for help and guidance, for healing and inspiration and for world peace. You can also seek guidance in everyday life and for personal spiritual awareness.

Guardian Spirits

Guardian spirits are to do with protection. Not everyone has a guardian spirit. This is not because they don't deserve them, it may be that they don't need them in this life or at this time in their life.

Guardians tend to work with spirits known as the Lords of Karma. They have a direct interest in caring for the planet and reinforcing the natural spiritual laws which underpin all of life. An example is St Peter at heaven's gate, who can send a soul up towards heaven or down towards hell! You will see examples of these characters in all world religions and belief systems. Lords of Karma can work with people such as ghost busters, exorcists, priests, medicine men and women, high lamas and so on. In general, they are those who guide the dead into the other world. They protect the higher realms from being polluted by the lower spirits.

Doorkeepers also come into this category. They are spirits who protect your psychic doorways into the spirit world – you could call them psychic bouncers. They are tough, discriminating and are working in psychic capacity to protect you.

Why Do Guides Come into Our Lives?

Guides come for specific purposes, and will remain until that purpose is fulfilled. Some will appear just once, if once is sufficient to bring information, comfort and healing. Occasionally a guide can appear as an archetype – a goddess, god or a mythological figure – or even as a fairy or pixie. They can appear as a Christian saint, if that is what you need to see. Relatives appear frequently as guides, whether it's a grandmother or a deceased spouse or son, a distant mother or an unborn infant.

A guide takes you on the first part of your life's journey. In some cases you will have the same guide throughout your life, in other cases they hand over the responsibility to another guide until we reach our full capacity of spiritual learning and then we have earned the right to be working with higher guides who are part of the angelic ministry.

Most people are not aware that they are there and find that as soon as they open up to the spirit world, either through psychic development or just by being spiritually aware, they appear.

There are also master guides who are not in contact with the living as regularly as the spirit guides. They watch over higher development, and great advances of thinking, evolution and spirituality. When someone experiences a life-threatening situation or crisis that threatens their ability to succeed in their life's destiny, it is the master guide who comes to the rescue and saves the day. These spirits are aides and supporters of people working for a divine purpose. When perceived in meditation they appear more often as beings of light rather than in human or animal form.

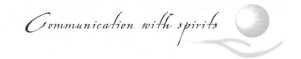

Meeting Your Spirit Guide

The psychic centre used to communicate with the spirit world is at a sensitive point at the base of the skull through which we connect to energies coming from our environment and astral world. This is where many spirits communicate with the living, whether ancestors, deceased friends, relatives or earthbound entities. This is the place where we dream into the spirit world.

In general, we sense the energies in the atmosphere through our emotional mind in the solar plexus but this doorway is used when we are learning how to develop psychic skills to communicate with the spirit world, but also to communicate visions and psychic impressions.

If you really want to know who your guiding spirit is, a simple ritual or ceremony can bring that connection into your life. Choose a night of the full moon to conduct this ritual (a full moon is ideal for opening psychic energy) and decide whether you want to conduct it alone or with like-minded friends who are also seeking a heartfelt connection to spirit.

I always recommend that you have spent time learning how to use your psychic skills before you move forward into the area of spirit communication because the reality is that not all spirits are benevolent (see section on psychic protection).

Preparation

Choose a room or place in your garden or on your balcony from where the moon is in plain view. If the moon is obscured by clouds do not attempt to make the connection. Also avoid it if you are not feeling well within yourself and everything seems to make you feel ungrounded or chaotic. This may be a sign that the spirit world does not want to reveal itself to you at this time or you may not be emotionally ready. In this case the ritual should be put off until a time with favourable omens.

Don't communicate with the spirit world on an empty or full stomach, or having had too much to drink – and avoid drugs or smoking too much. Your clothes should be plain and simple and make sure you are not wearing a heavy belt or jewellery, as this will break the flow of energy in your body, which needs to be comfortable and unhindered.

Achieving contact with the spirit world is not dissimilar to a meeting of two factions wishing to conduct mutual business negotiations; each must go half way to make it happen – bringing the physical world and the spirit world into juxtaposition.

There is a place inside everybody where all voices come to rest; a twilight zone of silence, a place the scientists call the 'alpha' state of mind. That state is ideal for communicating with spirits and you will need to reach this state before you begin to make it happen. In Spiritualist associations, meetings often begin with a prayer and communal meditation. This raises the vibrational level of the atmosphere in the room where they are conducting spirit communication so that it is high enough to be touched by the angels and higher beings.

The practical reason for this is that the spirit world is filled with many kinds of spirit beings both of a higher vibrational level – therefore higher beings – and others who are more corrupt or earthbound, who draw from the astral levels and can cause harm to the living. Never underestimate the power of spirit, particularly if you invite them into your life without ensuring protection and guidance.

Meeting Your Spirit Guide

- Ensure the room where you will conduct the ritual is clean, calm and lit only by candles. Switch off any electrical equipment. If the room contains your altar, place a gift to your spirit guide on the altar such as flowers or food. Light a candle in a colour that you think represents your guide. You maybe surprised how much you know about them already …

- Light some incense, again choose a fragrance that you think represents your guide.

- Choose the right time. Obviously it has to be night time as you need the light of the full moon, but the best time is midnight. The evening is also acceptable as the night brings in the right peaceful atmosphere.

- Lie down or sit up in a meditation pose, either on a chair or on the floor with cushions. You should be comfortable and therefore able to relax and concentrate.

- Begin with a prayer to the spirit world asking for guidance and help in meeting your spirit guide. Now relax your mind and body with a simple relaxation meditation. Release any fears you have about connecting with the spirit world. The spirit world is generally very wise and compassionate; it will not reveal itself to you if you are not ready for it. Everything in existence, whether spirit or not spirit, will treat you with care and intelligence if you are sincerely seeking to better yourself and to grow in understanding and love.

- As you close your eyes call upon the spirit protectors and ask them to show you your guide. Connect with your heart and feel your spirit guide connect into your heart chakra. Close your eyes and follow the rhythm of your breath, imagine your breath to be the waves of the sea gently breaking on the shore, one following the other, one merging into the other. As you dissolve into a state of pure relaxation, you will feel the love and healing energy of your spirit guide and gradually you can build a vision in your mind of what they are like – it could be a face, or a form, or the way they are dressed, what they are holding in their hands, etc.

- Sometimes, after a period of meditating on your spirit guide, more than one guide appears. This can be confusing, so ask your life guide to appear first, and the others to wait until you are ready. Meeting one at a time is sufficient until you are a little more experienced and confident in what you pick up psychically.

Impressions and responses come in a number of ways, mostly sensory. You may see your guide visually, or hear telepathically, experience a powerful fragrance, a touch sensation, a feeling of stationary presence or supernatural occurrences. It can feel as simple as an intuition of someone being there with you, someone known and loved. Guides can appear as light or more usually as male or female; your own psychic receptivity gives them their appearance and gender, as light is their actual form. When you feel them come ask their name and trust what you feel.

Such a meeting can be very positive and a happy experience. Once you have seen there is a presence which is there just for you, helping and guiding you, it will give you a feeling of 'having a friend' that will stay with you forever. I find that when I am really struggling with my life, or I am exhausted, I can go into my room and connect with my guides to ask for healing or guidance … they always come when asked.

'My ancestors and spirit guides make it crystal clear to me that they are ever by my side. They are always there to take me by the hand and lead me.' Rhona, businesswoman

Strengthening the Connection

Once you have made the connection with your spirit guide you will want to maintain the link. Your connection with your guide can be maintained and strengthened in a number of ways.

- First you need to visualize him or her as you first saw them when they came to you. To build a stronger image of them each time you link in ask yourself, are they tall, dark, fair? What nationality are they? What are they wearing? Do they have long hair or short? Do they wear a hat or headdress? What colour are their robes/clothes? Concentrate in your mind's eye on each feature and the details of your guide's dress. 'Hear' a voice with its special accent, emphasis on certain words and idiosyncrasies of speech.

- If you should sense a negative figure or resistances or blocks, go deeper into the meditative state and try sending the resistance away like soft clouds moving away from you, and return to connecting. You may find that your mood or energy when trying to connect might be affected by your day, so clearing your chakras or aura before you meditate with your guide will certainly help your mood. It may take a few nights of trying to connect before anything appears, but don't be disheartened, it is worthwhile working at it until you find that connection. Sometimes you may need to look at how relaxed you are, or how fully grounded you are feeling? It may be the wrong time to connect or the wrong day.

- Find out as much as you can about your guide's culture. Read any literature, visit museums, read biographies or, if you have the chance, visit the country they are from.

- Gradually isolate your main guide (as many mediums and psychics have a number of spirits who work together). When you know who is in charge make them responsible for sorting out the pecking order within your guides and spirit helpers.

- When you go to sleep, hold the image of your spirit guide in your mind's eye as you drift into dreams. As you wake, draw the image close in your semi-conscious awareness. Gradually the figure will begin to speak and to act as a guide through your dreams, and eventually start to occasionally appear in your waking world. They will gradually speak to your own inner voice or with a strong feeling; it takes time and confidence to discover how they access you on a conscious level.

- Begin to question your guide further. Ask why he or she is there, what is his or her purpose in being with you. Ask each question over a several meditations until you feel safe and confident with the answers. You can then ask about the lifetime that he or she appears from and in what other lives you have known each other.

- It is helpful to keep a record of the messages that you get from your guide and the development of your relationship. Try accessing this information through the subconscious mind as channelled material – also called automatic writing. This may take some time but gradually your confidence in the connection will grow and you will find the medium you are supposed to work with in the future with your guide.

Accepting a spirit guide does not mean that you give up your autonomy. Guides are there only to advise; they cannot and do not make choices or force you to accept theirs. The majority of guides interact with you in a friendly relationship and with the same type of interactions as friends or family who you are close to and love.

I have found working with guides to be one of the most rewarding aspects of psychic development and of connecting with God/divine. They have given me the belief that I am loved, wanted and protected, cared about and supported in all I do.

Your Sacred Relationship with Your Spirit Guides

I recommend to many of my clients when they know who is guiding them – particularly if it is a relative that they knew – that they place a photograph of them in the home and, from time to time, light a candle for them and place fresh flowers near their picture. You can do this on your altar or sacred space at home or at work. If a picture isn't appropriate, you can place a symbol that represents them in your life, such as Buddha if they are Buddhist, or an artifact from Africa if they are African, or Aboriginal if they are from Australia, and so on.

Every day you can ask them for advice and help with your day-to-day life. Also ask for their help and support when you are very worried, ill or something has happened to someone you love. It is more powerful to go straight to the divine source but when that appears too difficult for you to manage then your guide is like your connection to the divine or like a father or mother figure offering love, support and help.

Angela Watkins, a well-known London-based medium, has several guides but she knows that if she calls them collectively the right one for the right job will turn up. 'They work in mysterious ways. When you think that there is no one out there and you are filled with grief or despair – it is at these darkest moments that you realize that you are not alone and that there is a greater force of love and compassion out there in the universe to help and guide you. I give thanks to my guides every day for their patience and kindness in looking after my family and me. God bless them.'

Dangers

As spirit communication involves probing a world that is scarcely understood even by the most dedicated spiritualist, it is not an art to learn with enthusiastic friends by summoning spirits into a candle flame or holding a séance to attract entities from another world. There is a universal understanding in all cultures and religions that there are good and bad spirits. I know of individuals and psychic development groups who have strayed into the business of spirit contact and rescue and found themselves haunted by malevolent spirits. Always practise spirit communication in a safe and secure environment.

Communicating with spirits takes time and experience to learn in a safe and secure way. Medicine men and shamans take years to study their art form and have a mentor or teacher to guide them through their early years until they are able to stand up to the pressure of spirit communication.

There are some guides who you may not feel safe with. In this case you have the authority to ask them to leave. A guide that appears at a time when you don't want to communicate can be asked to come back later. Sometimes guides are sent to help you realize things you don't want to see or make changes you need but are resisting. Be aware of what's really good for you before refusing the presence of a guide showing unwanted truths. Always trust your instinct if you are ever unhappy with a spirit who has come to work with you or who you suspect of not being as supportive as they make out.

A few pranksters and negative characters can slip through the net – mainly as a lesson for us in understanding that not all aspects of the spirit world are made in heaven – but simply refusing it, breaking the contact or asking it to leave tends to be sufficient to release the entity from your life. When spirits claim to be Joan of Arc or Henry VIII they are usually pranksters and very rarely the real thing.

Mediumship

Connecting with a spirit guide is something most of us can achieve, and it can be an invaluable source of guidance in our personal lives. Mediumship takes the connection with the spirit world to a more philanthropic level.

Mediums are men and women who have the ability to contact people who have died and, by using various psychic skills such as clairaudience, clairsentience and clairvoyance, to communicate advice, warnings and wisdom from the spirit world. There are many examples of famous mediums – such as Doris Stokes who gave mass demonstrations at huge venues or the American medium Jane Roberts who channelled the wisdom and insight of the entity Seth – but there are also many mediums who operate through the Spiritualist associations, psychic colleges and Spiritualist churches.

It is said that mediums are born, not made, and many mediums will have experienced psychic phenomena since early childhood. For others, it is a gift that does not emerge until adulthood, perhaps triggered by a bereavement or serious illness. The majority of people who are fascinated by psychic studies will have some natural mediumistic ability, but few choose to develop their abilities formally as it requires a willingness to learn in a structured way how to communicate with other dimensions and a commitment to the long and sometimes slow process of working within a psychic development group.

How Spirit Communication Works

Mediums learn to tune into other dimensions so that they can seek contact with a deceased relative on behalf of a living family member. In reality their request for such contact will not always be granted. A medium should not be judged on how good or bad they are according to their ability to communicate with a person on the other side, as the deceased spirit may not wish to talk or may be unable to.

An Irish family contacted me a few years ago: three girls in their late teens, whose mother had died quite suddenly of breast cancer. The three sisters all came to see me, desperate to communicate with their mother. However, she would not come, preferring instead to send her own mother. Their grandmother came to talk to the girls, to tell them that their mother was not ready to speak as she was still experiencing very powerful emotions – she was still missing her physical life and in particular her girls.

Many years later – once the girls were older and had their own families – they returned to see me. As soon as they arrived I felt a female presence. Her energy was so light and peaceful it placed me in a serene space. It was their mother. They were delighted to know that she was there but, coincidentally, the middle sister had been dreaming about her since the birth of her own daughter so we concluded that their mother had chosen to come to guide the little girl.

Good mediums have a highly developed psychic awareness and therefore often pick up information about people they meet in daily life. They will also pick up messages from the spirit world even when they are not linking in. However, on a conscious level, most mediums function entirely in the physical world: they are concerned with families, mortgages or rent, shopping and business, just like anyone else. It is crucial that the physical reality of daily life remains as important as the spiritual one. Becoming too involved in psychic activity can usurp the material world, causing the psychic to become ungrounded and open to uncontrolled mediumship. This is a serious danger for the trainee; becoming too open to the spirit world without protection and guidance can, in extreme cases, cause mental instability with mild psychosis and depression. It must be taken very slowly and always with the correct intention.

It is also vital to close down and ground your psychic energies when you come back to physical reality. This does not need to be anything complicated. One medium I know finds that simply lighting a cigarette gives them the chance to ground and close down their heart

chakra. I am not recommending that you start smoking to help ground your psychic energies but everyone finds their own method of switching off from the spirit world. I enjoy a cup of real coffee, while another friend who works as a clairvoyant and healer enjoys going to the gym after a long day with clients.

Different Forms of Psychic Communication with Spirits

The majority of professional mediums remain fully conscious during a sitting or public demonstration and many carry out spiritual healing using spirit guides. In the past many spiritualists used planchettes, a form of ouija board with a pencil attached to write down spirit messages. They also relied on the old methods of table tapping for yes and no or holding seances where spirits were called down to communicate and manifest to the living.

Spirit communication is for many a religion, a calling. At Spiritualist church services, psychic development circles and seances the communication begins with prayers to God. All mediums believe in Spirit, a divine power that guides them, although in modern times, as with other religions, the strict rules of Spiritualism are not followed to the letter by those who may embrace a wider belief system.

The most common type of spirit communication is overshadowing. This is when the medium or clairvoyant remains conscious throughout and the spirit doesn't enter them but sits or stands inside their aura. They then sense or hear the spirit communicate with them and translate what is being said to the audience.

When I communicate with spirits, they usually come and sit in my aura, generally on my right-hand side, and I can hear them talking to me just behind my right ear. If I am able to see spirit it is as if I am looking through lace curtains and seeing first a shadow then a more focused image of how they look, how tall they are, what they are wearing, etc. I can see them just out of the corner of my right eye.

Over the years I have met many channels who are able to bring the spirit right inside their bodies and become unconscious of the spirit communication, as part of their conscious mind links into the spirit world. These mediums are referred to as trance mediums. They usually have spirit guides through which they communicate, linking them to higher or even lower spirit levels. In some cases they fall into a deep trance state similar to being hypnotized. With

transfiguration mediumship the spirit communicator takes on the face and sometimes the voice of a deceased person, and even manifests the form of the spirit in a mist, standing beside them, as their voice changes into that of his or her guide.

A direct voice medium is able to allow a spirit to talk through her voice box with the spirit's own voice but they do not manifest spirit, the spirit speaks through them using their own voice.

Beginning Your Journey as a Spirit Communicator

One of the best ways to learn how to communcate with spirits is through a psychic development or mediumship workshop. Whether you are already in contact with your spirit guides or not, you will find it very useful in gaining confidence. I have found, over the years, that the best mediums and spirit communicators are not always the best teachers, so attend classes that are popular with students of the psychic arts and recommended by people that you trust.

Once you have learnt how to spirit communicate you may wish to take it further by acting as a medium for others. There are safe environments where you can practise this. Spiritualist churches, for instance, offer space for students to practise on an audience, while colleges that teach psychic development will have open days where you go along and try out your skills. As they say, practice makes perfect, and the more you do the better you will become at it and gradually your confidence will grow.

Always remember, however, that you will pick up a lot of psychic and emotional energy from spirit communication. Before I begin a session, apart from linking with my God, I always call my main guide to protect and guide the session and ensure that the spirits who come don't leave any residual psychic and emotional energy that may affect me. Protection is important for those who communicate with the psychic realms, so we will look at various methods in the next section.

Psychic protection

Everyone, at some time in their life, needs psychic protection. This is not some strange form of magic but simply a barrier that protects us from other people's thoughts and feelings.

The key to psychic protection is self-awareness. The less we know about ourself the more vulnerable we are to psychic attack. Such attacks can begin with letting people bully us. This weakens our defences, breaking down our self-confidence and, therefore, our protection. Self-knowledge strengthens our immunity, enabling psychic influences to bounce off and, in some cases, return to the sender. Psychic attack is not necessarily a great occult mystery conducted by magicians and witches, although they are the experts. We can take on board subliminal messages from advertising, telephone and Internet communications and letters, photographs, gifts – any object that carries an atmosphere that is not conducive to our energy.

Giving too much of yourself away is one of the key areas of psychic weakness, particularly at work and in relationships. Whenever you become depleted after being with a particular person – or in a certain atmosphere or place – it is worthwhile asking yourself the following:

- Have I become too sympathetic to that person and their circumstances?
- Have I taken on something from that person?
- Am I allowing them to have undue influence over me?
- After a telephone call to a friend, a member of my family or a client do I feel drained or affected by their personality?

- Do I take on other people's personalities like a sponge and cannot detach myself from their energy?
- Do particular places affect me?
- Do I get depleted when travelling by public transport?
- Do I get depleted in crowded places such as shopping malls and nightclubs?

If you answer yes to any of these questions then you need to consider practising psychic protection in your daily life. Many people believe that psychic protection is not for them because they don't see ghosts, or upset anyone enough to provoke psychic attack, or just do not do anything as occultist and strange as psychic protection. However, it can be in the small, everyday areas of life that psychic protection is most needed, yet not practised.

The magical arts of serious psychic protection are only necessary when you come across an evil or malevolent force either from a person, a cult or a place. If you do come under this type of psychic attack or experience you are usually aware of this and know that you need to defend yourself.

It is the more subtle areas of psychic energy – the thoughts, feelings, atmospheres and emotions of people – that affect your daily life. This can leave you feeling exhausted, depleted (both mentally and physically) and imposed upon.

Creating Protective Boundaries

Learning simple techniques off by heart will help you create protective boundaries. These techniques include opening and closing your chakras, shielding and protecting your energy, knowing how to ground yourself and recognizing when to open up to other people's emotions or when to remain detached and closed to their influence.

Psychic protection is vital in psychic development as there are dangers in opening up to the spirit world and to psychic energy. The term 'uncontrolled psychic' is banded about in psychic circles to refer to a gifted person who has opened too quickly and too early in their career as a psychic. This creates an uneven development in the natural progress of opening up to a more sensitive level of being. Without being able to ground or protect themselves, the novice psychic can experience a rush of psychic energy and messages that can lead to a state of confusion, mental disturbance, insomnia and uncontrolled attacks.

Taking Care of Body and Mind

Prosaic as it may seem it is important to get adequate sleep, rest and relaxation. Most of us feel more vulnerable when we are stressed or tired, and we become more sensitive to any kind of pressure. If we become too vulnerable we can sense people's moods too easily. This can be overwhelming and leave you feeling oversensitive and exhausted. And if you're exhausted, you're psychically vulnerable.

We need rest and a healthy lifestyle to ensure a strong psychic constitution. If our physical nervous systems are weak our psychic system will be weak too. Physical health and psychic health are interlinked: if your nervous system is exhausted, you can easily be overwhelmed by changes in your energy field that would normally cause you no tension or difficulty at all. Check your sleeping patterns; your consumption of alcohol, drugs, cigarettes and caffeine; manage your time better and commit less to overworking – even if it means reining in your ambition a little. Use sensible strategies to live a healthy and humane lifestyle.

The Key to Protection is Grounding

Grounding yourself provides a stable psychic foundation upon which to rest your mind while enabling it to be free at the same time. Being grounded is about being dynamically focused in the body. There is a sense of 'presence' as psychic energy flows from the more subtle levels of the psyche into our physical body. We can be focused and get on with the task in hand.

When we're ungrounded we're cut off from our body and are therefore unaware of the body's needs. The energy circuit is incomplete and the auric field is greatly weakened. In this state we become anxious and are more easily influenced by the thoughts and emotions of others.

Your Feet

Without feet you would lose your ability to stand, walk, run, cycle and balance. Your feet provide you with the basis for all upright action, supporting your journey in life. Keep your attention on your feet next time you meditate, dance, walk in the countryside, run or work out.

Grounding Exercise

- Remove all footwear and any socks or tights. Stand comfortably with your feet shoulder-width apart, weight evenly distributed between left and right feet, with the outside of your feet parallel and facing forwards. Bend your knees slightly and tuck your tailbone in. Straighten your back and tuck your chin in slightly. Spread your toes as wide as you can, stretching the balls of your feet.

- Gently press your weight into the balls of your feet and imagine that you are pushing your toes into the earth. Gently move your weight so you are pushing down through your heels into the earth. Now centre your weight so it is evenly distributed in the centre of both feet.

- Breathe deeply and imagine that your energy is sinking into the ground, into the warm moist earth. Breathe out the energy that is blocking your movement down into the earth – this is emotional energy trapped in the chest or head area. Then again breathe deeply and move your focus down into the earth.

- As you begin to sink down connect up with a golden light that is living and breathing within the earth. Bring this energy up inside your body from your feet and up through the front of your body into each nerve end and chakra point, cleansing and energizing as you move up to the crown of your head. Now imagine the golden energy moving down the back of your head, down your spine back in to the earth.

- To finish, wiggle your toes in the earth and breathe slowly in and out. Open your eyes and relax. You should feel energized and grounded.

Note: Sinking into the earth is not the same as losing yourself to a heavy crumpling feeling. There is nothing to fear in sinking as the downward pull towards the earth is always counterbalanced by the upward pull of your spirit vitality towards universal energy. You sense this energy through the crown chakra, which is essential in maintaining the connection with divine energy.

Quick-fix Grounding Exercises

- Imagine a camera lens bringing you into sharp focus
- Imagine roots growing out of the bottom of your feet and sinking deep into the earth
- Imagine a magnetic force pulling down on the base of your feet
- Stamp your feet and pat your body all over
- Imagine your consciousness coming in through the top of your crown and going down into your feet and filling you up like a glass of sparkling, cool water being poured

Protective Barriers

There are various types of protective barrier. These can be used for simple everyday protection or when working psychically.

The Psychic Bubble

This is most appropriate for use in everyday situations. We all have testing moments in our daily lives, be it going into a meeting where someone may be hostile or visiting a busy night-club or exhibition where so many competing energies can leave you exhausted. This simple technique involves creating a protective 'skin', a giant psychic membrane that protects you from negative vibrations coming from people or places. The power of protection is set in motion simply by visualizing it. Before trying this technique make sure that you are grounded and safe with the idea of being inside yourself – and that you are powerful enough to challenge any situation as psychic protection is also about confidence and faith.

Visualizing a Psychic Bubble

- Relax into your comfortable position, either in a chair or lying on the floor. Breathe and relax your mind and body. Begin your visualization. Imagine that you are surrounded by a transparent protective skin like a bubble or egg around your body. The nucleus of this egg is in your Hara point, which is just below your navel. It is the power base for your physical and spiritual vitality.

- Spend a while sensing the bubble of energy all around you, over your head, under your feet protecting your back and down your legs – completely surrounding you.

- Sense that your own vibrations can exit through the membrane of the bubble. Sense that the bubble does not prevent good energies coming in. Be relaxed and comfortable inside your self, have a clear perception that any unpleasant or negative external energies cannot penetrate. You can also fill the protective bubble with images that you like and feel will protect you, such as the symbol of the cross, star of David, Hindu symbol for aum, or images of sacred religious figures such as Jesus Christ, Buddha, Kuan Yin, etc.

- When you have made your bubble, exhale slowly and sense that your own warm breath carries your pure essence into the bubble, fill your bubble with your own vibration, do this for several breaths and relax into yourself …

Once set up, this bubble remains in a latent state until you activate it with visualization power. Once you have developed the intent to see this protective energy around you, you can bring in that protection whenever you need it.

The best time to set up the protection is in the morning, then give it a quick once over every few hours. Check it just before sleep and clear away any negative energy you may have picked up in your aura during the day. A bath or yogic breathing exercises are usually powerful enough to clear superficial psychic energy that has built up around your aura (this usually feels like a heaviness or tiredness around your back, neck and solar plexus). Visualize a strong green light pass over your entire body whilst lying in the bath or in bed relaxing. This can melt away any residual negative energy in your aura.

Shields

A shield is probably the most common form of protection and is found in many traditions. People usually place shields over the part of the body that feels most sensitive. In most cases this will be one or more of the chakras. For instance, if you are dealing with someone who has negative emotional energy, the solar plexus chakra should be protected by a shield; if someone is sending negative mental energy, then the third eye chakra benefits from protection. I was taught to use a shield made of mirror glass and sense that the shield reflects whatever atmosphere is coming at me back to the sender. Other examples of shields are the use of jewellery and amulets.

Visualizing fire or the image of a flame can also be useful, particularly if you wish to extend your personality or power into a given situation. You simply imagine that you are a vibrant burning flame and that the base of the flame is deep in the earth while your body is the core of the fire – so all bad thoughts and feelings burn up and melt as they come towards your radiance and charm!

The cloak is another common method of protection. This is ideal if you are working psychically – as a finishing sentiment when you close down. You just envelop yourself with a magic cloak. It may be a simple dark cloak, beautifully bright or even multicoloured. Draw it all around you, beginning at your head and shoulders and then down to the ground.

Closing down with a lead curtain is ideal for working or living with people whose energies drain you. Build up an image of a curtain hanging between you and the other person, making sure the curtain goes into the floor and up to the ceiling. Now begin to sense that it is made

of lead. Breathe gently and on the out-breath feel the warmth of your breath creating the curtain's density and physical form. It is a lead weight that nothing can penetrate, so all the demands of other people bounce off.

Other Means of Protection

Essential oils and crystals are a useful addition to the methods discussed above and are particularly suited to day-to-day use.

Essential Oils

If you're having any difficulty with a particular part of your body you can assess which chakra you feel is affected and apply the protective oil that corresponds to that chakra. Please note however that fragrances can evoke memories so please choose an oil which you intuitively sense is okay for you right now.

- *Neroli* (Crown)
  Embraces and transforms, reducing fear, shock and negative emotions.
- *Pine* (Third eye)
  Cleanses negativity from your aura and environment.
- *Peppermint* (Throat)
  Clears negativity from your aura and environment and reduces hysteria and shock.
- *Lavender* (Heart)
  Psychic first aid. Clears negativity and opens your crown chakra increasing your inner guidance.
- *Marjoram* (Solar Plexus)
  Calms a turbulent mind and emotions. Reduces psychic sensitivity, avoiding overload.
- *Benzoin* (Sacral)
  Balances your base and crown chakra and cleanses negativity from your aura and environment.
- *Patchouli* (Root)
  Grounds, centres and strengthens the base and sacral chakra.

Amulets

Throughout history, and in all cultures, amulets have been and still are used. An amulet is a defence, a charm of protection, worn to ward off evil and bad luck. Amulets come in many different forms from crystals and rocks to sacred writings and symbols. Many were designed to protect against the evil eye, deflecting it back at the sender. One potent form of deflection was the use of a grotesque head like a gargoyle, often found on the roofs of medieval churches and stately homes. Amulets in the form of eyes based on the eye of Horus were painted on ancient pottery and are still seen on the prows of boats in the Mediterranean.

Crystals are now the most popular form of amulet as they are portable and easy to wear. As well as offering protection, they can provide a general sense of calm and confidence to the wearer. For psychic protection wear tourmaline around the neck. For grounding try holding a boji stone in one or both hands or carry Jet.

CRYSTALS FOR PROTECTING AND ENERGIZING THE CHAKRAS
- *Base chakra:* black tourmaline, obsidian, bloodstone
- *Sacral chakra:* azurite, golden topaz
- *Solar plexus chakra:* malachite, jasper, tiger's eye
- *Heart:* rose quartz, aventurine, amazonite
- *Throat chakra:* turquoise, aquamarine, blue topaz, blue tourmaline
- *Third eye:* sodalite, azurite, lapis lazuli,
- *Crown chakra:* citrine, quartz and amethyst

Asking for Help

Whatever protective technique you use, it can be made much more effective if you also plug into a higher spiritual energy. Calling on the power of God or a religious icon is obviously easier to do if you have a religious background or spiritual experience. Learning how to have faith in a higher power can come easily if you open your mind to the idea that there is a universal energy that you can draw from whenever you require that extra strength or courage.

By sending out a thought, a prayer, through ritual or incantation, you can call upon the power of Divine/God. Open your heart and mind to receive this support and you will find an overwhelming, peaceful energy that will calm and centre you.

It is useful to experiment with the spiritual gateways that work best for you. Take a few moments to think of a symbol, a place or a being that represents that religious or divine inspiration. This may be a religious figure or a sacred place – a place where you feel you touch the Divine/God.

Close your eyes and bring that image closer to your body and mind and feel yourself being engulfed by the image, being touched by the religious icon and receiving healing and peace. If you are at a sacred place in nature, become a part of that place – open to the spiritual gateway and bring that power through your body and mind. Let it become a part of your inner sanctum that you can call upon whenever you are threatened, in fear or extreme emotion. You will find that the inner core begins to heal and calm your state of mind … try it and see.

Opening and Closing the Chakras

One of the basic lessons in psychic protection is to monitor and control the opening and closing of the chakras, so you bring them under conscious direction. There are times when it is appropriate to have your chakras open and times when it is important to have them closed, so you must learn the difference between the two and assess which is appropriate in any given situation.

If you find it difficult to visualize your chakras and whether they are open or closed, a pendulum can be used to dowse the energy of each chakra (see pages 64– 5). However, it is possible to train yourself to see or sense the chakras. Chakras that are open tend to be exceptionally bright, rotating at a fast rate and may feel hot and energized. Chakras that are closed have much less light and may appear like closed grey shadows in the aura. They tend to rotate much slower and may feel cold and lacking in energy.

It is possible to sense the chakras with the palm of your hand and feel a tingling sensation when the chakra is open and less so when it is closed. Also, you may find that a particular chakra is sending out more or less energy than the others. This normally suggests that there may be an imbalance or it is overactive due to blocked energy.

When dowsing the chakras to check whether they are open or closed you programme the pendulum by simply requesting that it 'check whether the chakras are open or closed'. The pendulum should rotate one way for yes and the other for no, so obviously you have to know which is which for your pendulum. The easiest way to find out is to hold the pendulum over the palm of your hand and ask 'Is my name …?' The movement should indicate yes. Now give an incorrect name to discover your no.

In general, when you check over each chakra a fast spin indicates that the chakra is open and a slower rotation indicates that it is closed. After a few weeks of practice you will be able to tell which one is still vibrating and open just by focusing on each chakra with your mind.

Opening and Closing the Chakras Exercise

- Make sure you are sitting or lying down comfortably. Keep your back straight with neck and head relaxed.

- Close your eyes and establish a gentle breathing rhythm.

- Take your attention to your chakras lined up through your body like round coloured lights.

- Take your attention down to the base of your spine. See your base chakra and visualize a whirling vortex of energy. Now picture this spin slowing down and imagine a wooden door closing over the front of the chakra and shutting in the light.

- Practise opening and closing the door a few times until it becomes automatic. You will know the difference within your body as the chakra opens and closes.

- Take your attention to the sacral chakra two inches below your navel and see the whirling vortex of energy and light, then close the door across the chakra and shut in the light.

- Bring your attention to your solar plexus chakra and visualize the whirling vortex of energy and light, then close the door across the chakra and shut in the light.

- Move up to the heart chakra. Again visualize the whirling vortex of light and then close the door across the chakra, shutting in the light.

- Take your attention to the throat chakra and see the vortex of whirling energy and light, close the door across the chakra, shutting in the light.

- Move up to the third eye chakra, see the vortex of energy and light, close the door across the chakra and shut in the light.

- Finally, move up to the top of your head to the crown chakra, see the vortex of light and energy, bring the door across the chakra and sense as it closes that you have shut in the light.

- Now take your attention to your feet and feel the earth beneath you. Open your eyes and take a deep breath.

- Stand up and feel your feet firmly on the floor. Have a good stretch and know that you are grounded.

Once you are confident you can open and close your chakras at will, try running up and down your spine assessing the state of the chakras. You can then send healing energy into the chakra which appears depleted or imbalanced.

You may find that in certain situations you automatically cover a specific chakra with your hands or arms because you feel vulnerable in that area. This most commonly happens with the solar plexus when you are in the company of someone you feel uncomfortable with or threatened by; and with the throat chakra when you feel insecure about your communication skills. The best thing to do is work through your insecurities but, before they can be healed, you must ensure that you build up shields of psychic protection in the areas of vulnerability until you are confident that you are safe.

Know the Enemy Within

Part of the work with psychic protection is to heal what is within us waiting to be healed. This gives strength and confidence in our ability to utilize psychic protection tools. Instead of using up much-needed energy defending ourselves from something within, we need to strengthen ourselves to cope with outside influences that cause us stress, psychic attack and disturbance.

Psychic protection is very useful for providing space to deal with a difficult situation but we must not ignore or further repress wounds that need healing. Psychologically, we have all been wounded in some way. These wounds are often repressed so that we no longer remember them, but they sit in the unconscious mind and emotions. (Shamans call this unconsciousness soul loss.) These repressed parts are not just 'in the mind', but are energy forms held in the aura without recognition – and these energy forms can cause illness and stress.

It is important to have some understanding of the energies within our personality. We are often attacked by our own inner shadows, repressed parts of the psyche, and we then blame other people. It is important to become responsible for our own darkness. When we encounter an atmosphere we do not like, there is always the possibility that its source is in our own psyche and energy field (aura).

Past wounds, or soul loss, cause considerable damage to the aura. The gap between the soul and the body becomes like a tunnel or back yard where anyone can throw their rubbish or negativity. While this gap remains, even those who tirelessly seek help from healers will find that their problems never seem to heal or go away. The shadow is the aspect which holds our repressed fears and anxieties.

Imagine that you were victimized by someone when you were young and have blocked it from your memory. The experience of victimization would then sit within you as a pocket of unresolved energy. This energy may contain fear, anger, resentment and so on. It is there, but you are not conscious of it. Then one day life creates an opportunity to help bring this energy to the surface; a situation that triggers these feelings. This could happen at work with an aggressive boss, or when visiting family overseas or meeting up with a long-lost relative. When the feelings surface you do not know that they belong to you, so you blame something outside yourself.

We are usually surrounded by people, situations and environments that have similar psychological patterns and history to us. In many cases enemies at work, in the family or social groups tend to be people with similar energy to our own. Once you recognize the pattern and heal the unconscious energy, the relationship will also change for the better. We need to understand that we carry all kinds of unconscious patterns and defence mechanisms that sit as energies in our aura and are liable to be triggered by anyone with the same history.

In some cases meeting someone who reminds you of your abuser – whether that was a parent who was a little tough on you or someone who physically abused you – is enough for your own psychological process to throw up your repressed energy.

Accepting All Parts of the Whole

To be whole we have to accept all parts of ourselves and be in touch with all parts of our personality. When we go to healers and therapists to help us understand and identify our personality, the first step is to heal our wounds and call back parts of us that have been damaged. People ask me 'what sort of person am I?' Earthy, sensitive, artistic, powerful, loving … but there are never any 'right' answers. You cannot pick and choose the personality traits you like and put them all in a neat little box marked 'caring individual' or whatever. What is important is that we experience all aspects of who we are and learn not to judge ourselves too harshly.

This is difficult to do, particularly if we have internalized a lifetime of judgments from our parents, teachers, siblings, family and personal relationships. Samantha Jones, a London-based journalist, received a lot of criticism from her grandmother during her childhood and consequently, when she went to boarding school, she accepted harsh criticism from her teachers. Her educational life was as traumatic as her home-based childhood. This has lead her throughout her adult life to never feel that her work is adequate and to constantly seek the approval of others. 'When I hand in work to my editor I wait for some kind of rejection or criticism and when it doesn't happen and the feature is run in the paper, I feel that I have just climbed a hurdle. I know this insecurity stems from my childhood, even though I am happily married and successful.'

Releasing the Shadow

Only do this exercise when you feel ready to release your shadow – it is like having a spring clean of all old thoughts and memories. The recommended period for this exercise is from the autumn equinox on September 21 right up to the end of November, as this is a time of shedding and release.

- Choose a location where you are safe and comfortable. Ensure that it is at night and the room is dark except for the moonlight and/or a single candle.

- Lie down on the floor or ground and close your eyes. First conduct a relaxation meditation. If you begin to feel afraid it simply means that you are being receptive to the vibrations of your shadow and the moment of opening up has begun.

- As you are lying down on the ground, imagine that you are surrounded by a golden light – a sphere of gentle energy to calm and soothe you as you make your connection. If you are feeling agitated and worried do a simple breathing exercise: release all your fears by imagining you are exhaling grey clouds of fear and anxiety, and then breathing in light.

- Imagine a big sphere hovering above you. In that sphere you pack all your fears, your passions, your ideas, all the people who are attached to you and whom you are attached to. The sphere is tied to you with a silver cord, which you will imagine yourself breaking with the index and middle finger of your left hand. Some strange experiences can happen with this method of release. You might see in the sphere wild faces contorting and screaming, mouths shouting in anguish, or shouting in anger and ridicule. Or you might see strange symbols or geometrical figures; the sphere might expand more and more … You are putting your identity in that sphere, and there are facets of it of which you are not aware. So, angry, passionate people, whose emotions are hot, are likely to see their heat in the sphere. On the other hand the coldness of a methodical, calculating person might project them as an image of an icy ring inside the sphere. If there is one particular thing disturbing you at this moment in your life, it will certainly appear inside your sphere – this could be a person, a situation or even just an idea. It could be either plain and clear, such as someone's face, or a symbol. Don't try to understand the images, let them float in the sphere above you. Let them do what they want, and change as much as they like. A point will come when the activity inside the sphere begins to subside, and you will feel ready to cut the cord.

- Whatever images may come up, make sure they stay inside the sphere. If the image is outside in some way, put it back in. If you cannot do that for some reason, it is better to stop the experience as this may suggest that you either do not have sufficient awareness and control over yourself (therefore meeting with unfamiliar spiritual/psychic presences may actually be harmful). Or it may suggest that that image has a presence attached to it (such as a feeling of deep fear or anger) that suggests that you have a psychic attachment that is affecting your well-being – one which cannot be released by just placing it inside the sphere.

- You then need to cut the cord, realizing that it is your sphere with all your current fears and passions. It is your sphere created by your imagination, you are its master and you are the only person who can decide to set it free. You then send the sphere to the Divine/God who, like a father or mother, is able to help you release your shadow. The release of the sphere is to enable you to see the way life projects its fears and troubles and you carry them on your back like a heavy weight.

- Finally you send the sphere away from the earth towards the light of the Sun to be released as energy into the universe.

- Close down your meditation, bring your attention back into your body, wiggle your toes, take a deep breath and open your eyes. Realize that you are connected in your body and into the earth. Stretch and relax.

When you complete this exercise you will probably feel tired so go to bed and sleep. You should wake up in the morning with a focus on the future and on the positive areas of your life.

WARNING This is powerful meditation and should be conducted only when you are at ease with your psychic powers.

Useful tools

Crystals

Crystals can assist us to focus and amplify what we do with our minds, energies and willpower. Our bodies are controlled and regulated by different energies pulsating through them: crystals are tools to work with and influence those energies.

The use of crystals in healing is not a new phenomenon. The laying on of stones is an ancient art and today more and more people are rediscovering the wonders of crystal healing, as well as the value of crystals in enhancing the atmosphere of the home and creating a sense of well-being.

Types of Crystals

Diamonds, topaz, rubies, agate and quartz are among the most precious treasures to be found within the earth. From ancient times they have been extracted and worn to represent both material and spiritual wealth. Stones and crystals have always lent themselves as excellent tools of magic, psychic powers and healing.

The number of different kinds of precious and semi-precious stones available is enormous – too great to examine them all in this book. Instead, I have included a selection of the most commonly used crystals for enhancing your energy and protection, and for enhancing and clearing space in the home and at work.

Those which will work best for you, and in what area of your life, depends largely on your needs and what you want to use them for. You may not always agree with my interpretation of a crystal and how I would use it for psychic powers or protection, so use this as a guideline as you begin to develop your own magical relationship with them.

Quartz

As we look back through history the list of stones used as amulets and talismans is extensive. However, there is one stone that stands out from the rest, a stone that appears universally across many cultures, from Eskimos to the shamans of Malaysia and South America. It is the crystal of great magic, power and light – the clear quartz.

The quartz crystal is the most common crystal. It concentrates the rays of the sun and can therefore be used for magic, clearing space and for pendulums. Clear quartz is known as the energy stone because of its natural ability to absorb, store, amplify and transmit energy. It appears in a number of different forms.

CRYSTAL CLUSTERS

A crystal cluster consists of many crystals growing together from the same base. These crystals are very useful in a family home or a busy office, as they have a harmonizing and uplifting effect. Each cluster contains the polarities of negative and positive and in bigger clusters represent north, south, east and west. They clear air – almost like an ionizer that will recharge the atmosphere. I place clusters in offices, waiting rooms and living rooms – any-where where people congregate – to create harmony and balance. They are also wonderful in the garden.

TWIN CRYSTALS

Twin crystals tend to be equal in size, although sometimes one is much bigger than the other. They will help balance male and female energy as they symbolize the unification of ideals and the ability to merge with one another without the loss of power. This is ideal for couples or someone needing to unify the personalities at work.

LASER WAND CRYSTALS

These very powerful crystals, which look like Darth Vader's sword in *Star Wars*, can be used like a pair of scissors or a knife. They are particularly good for cutting through negative energy or for spiritual healing. They are also good for severing bonds that restrict and, because they shield a space from negative or intruding energy, they are extremely helpful with psychic protection – either for wearing or placing around a home or workplace.

Amethyst

This is one of the most beautiful varieties of quartz. Its shades vary from very dark violet to pale rose, with the darkest shades the most appreciated. This is the spiritual stone par excellence. It is often called the peace stone, as it is a good stone for meditation and spirituality. It makes an excellent crystal for the bedroom because of its calming qualities. The amethyst also has strong protective qualities. Many people wear it as a necklace or bracelet, or carry it in a pouch as protection against negative energy from other people – particularly the emotions of sadness or stress.

Rose Quartz

This is known as the love stone – the stone of the heart. It works on the emotions, helping to bring balance and harmony. It is the perfect stone for people who feel unloved, as its gentle calming influences help heal emotional wounds. It can be worn as a pendant over the heart to send the heart its healing qualities or it can be placed beside the bed. Even in a sitting room it will create a calming and warm atmosphere.

Smoky Quartz

This is perfect for grounding and balancing. It has strong protective qualities. The smoky quartz is a good stone for urban life, and whether you work from home or in the office it is essential to have one on your desk or area of work – particularly if you work with computers. Place the crystal where it can absorb and dissolve negative energies. It cleans away the negative blockages and allows the positive energies to take their place.

Citrine

Citrine is known as the stone of joy. It represents abundance on all levels and is particularly useful in business. The energies of citrine are warm and uplifting and it helps to focus the mind.

Aquamarine

The pretty blue aquamarine has a clear, very soothing, cool energy. The darker the colour, the more precious the stone – the dark blue ones are the most sought after. Aquamarine promotes clarity of mind and is especially helpful when this clarity has been impaired by a strong emotion, such as anger or fear. In this case just holding it in your hand and looking at it will help you regain your composure. It is also a good crystal for healing and is known to be a cleanser and purifier.

Agate

This stone comes in many different varieties of colour, patterns and opacity. It is an excellent energy booster, but its various forms have different energies and different ways of being used for psychic power, magic and healing.

AGATE GEODE This particular agate has the power to open your psychic powers; it is therefore a very important one to use when you begin your psychic development. You can keep it by your bedside to nourish those qualities while you sleep. It can be used in meditation and visualization techniques to enhance your ability to see into the spirit world.

BOTSWANA AGATE This is a gorgeous stone – I have one in our healing room. Botswana agate is not used for deep spiritual changes or space clearing exercises: it is an unobtrusive and natural crystal that brings a peaceful and happy energy and is uplifting when you're feeling depressed or low.

MOSS AGATE This crystal should be worn when you need peace of mind and at the end of a period of anxiety when things have been too much to bear. It is a good stone to wear for doing moon rituals, and to use for purifying energy.

BLUE-LACED AGATE This is one of my favourites because of its delicate, pretty blue colour, with soft veining running through it. This feminine stone can be used in many different ways, for example helping to heal relationships, bring a new love into your life, or to fill your heart with a soft, loving feeling.

Turquoise

This blue–green crystal was sacred to the Native Americans and has been used as a good luck charm since ancient times. The influence from this crystal is indeed powerful. Turquoise is a protective stone which sustains the peace and contentment of the spirit in the face of hurt and peril. You can use it in meditation when facing troubled times and when your inner peace is threatened. However, if you are already feeling bad, depressed or unwell it is best to use a bloodstone to relieve those symptoms before working with turquoise.

Jasper

One-coloured jasper is rare, as it is usually a mixture of colours. Red jasper is the most valued. This is the crystal of strong healthy feelings, of love and passion and strong emotions. Needless to say this is the stone (along with the ruby) to use in love magic. Those who have a cold heart (whether the coldness is due to an illness, a broken heart or inhibited sexual responses) and need warmth, wearing red jasper can encourage passion. If you are already passionate, red jasper will only encourage you to be overemotional.

Bloodstone

This crystal is a very dark deep red that looks almost black. It helps to overcome states of depression and melancholia that are due to a general lowering of the body's vital energy. It should be used carefully as it has a strong healing power – only use it when you need it and then put it safely away. It is like an injection of strength.

Tiger's Eye

This beautiful stone – resembling the eye of a tiger – gives confidence to those who wear it. It brings an understanding of oneself and the strength to express one's personality. This is a great stone to give to teenagers who are ready to become independent. It also offers psychic protection when worn as a pendant or carried in a pouch.

Crystals for Space Clearing

The following selection of crystals help with space clearing (see House Healing, page 146). Their energy supports the process of transforming negative energy into positive. Certain crystals also assist in protecting a room or property from external negative or intrusive energies – either from the landscape (ley lines and energy lines) or from psychic and emotional energy coming from a neighbour or neighbouring property.

OBSIDIAN

The obsidian crystal is born out of the volcanoes and is one of the best crystals to use for clearing space in the home. It protects and shields against negativity and is one of the most powerful grounding stones. It is also a 'teacher' stone – it reflects your inner pain and inadequacies to help you understand your own flaws and how to correct them.

TOURMALINE

This special crystal possesses similar properties to quartz. It comes in various colours from colourless to brown, pink, lilac, green and black. It is a stone of protection, warding off fear and negativity. Its protective energies instill confidence in the wearer and enhance understanding and inspiration.

ROCK SALT

This is an effective purificate for the home. The power of salt is derived in part from its crystalline structure. It has remarkable purifying properties and has traditionally been used in rituals for cleansing and purification of negative energy. Christians have always used it to bless and christen and they use it in their exorcism rites to expel evil spirits.

FLUORITE OCTAHEDRON

This interestingly shaped stone is the one of work and business enterprises. It will help you channel your energies in a productive way, and can be safely used whenever you are performing protection rituals at work. The fluorite is like a transmitter and channels the power into whatever you want to develop.

Crystals and Stones to Enhance your Psychic Powers

AZURITE: helps with compassion and extending the spirit of brotherhood and love. It provides stamina against weariness.

MOON STONE: the stone of the night. It enhances the night's gifts and brings in dreams and silence.

OPAL: a stone of spirits, it helps you get in touch with the spirit world.

QUARTZ: the energy stone, it aids concentration and healing magic.

SILVER: makes you appreciate purity and simplicity.

CALCITE: an energy amplifier, it is useful in directing energy. It also provides a barrier against negative energy.

MALACHITE: this stone of transformation assists in changing situations, clearing and activating the heart, and communication with spirit. It is an equalizing and balancing crystal.

HEMATITE: a stone for the mind, it enhances mental capability, calms atmospheres and assists in the focusing of energy and emotions for balance between body, mind and spirit. A good grounding crystal as it brings tranquillity and emotional clarity.

AMETHYST: a spiritual stone that develops and evolves spirituality. It helps meditation and can be used in dream magic.

SODALITE: an excellent stone for using in groups as it provides solidarity. It helps to eliminate confusion and stimulates the intellect.

DIAMOND: suggests indomitable strength and everlasting ties. It makes psychic power totally solid and lasting. Use with prudence.

JADE: (one of my favourites) brings beauty – the ability to recognize one's own beauty – and self love.

FLUORITE: increases the ability to concentrate, balances positive and negative aspects of the mind, increases the ability to see reality and truth – a stone of discernment and aptitude.

ROSE QUARTZ: appropriate in all healing rituals. It works very well with other crystals and opens you to a loving energy.

LAPIS LAZULI: a crystal for children – to guide and protect and improve child–adult relationships.

AMBER: allows the body to heal itself by absorbing and transmuting negative energy into positive energy. It is soothing, calming and enlivening; is excellent for realization and opens the spirit to unconditional love.

Healing/Protective Stones

TEKTITE: has banishing properties and sucks up bad energies so it can be used for protection against hatred, jealousy, envy and anger. It acts to balance the feminine and masculine properties in one's character.

SULPHUR: is negatively electrified so will assist in the removal of negative wilful energy from earthbound spirits, and eliminate negative thoughts from people in the home or workplace.

PETRIFIED WOOD: brings clarity and assists in establishing a natural order.

CARNELIAN AGATE: protects against envy, fear and rage and helps banish sorrow. An excellent crystal for cleansing negativity from other stones, and for directing energy in a place or property. Carnelian has been used with chlorite and ruby crystals to eliminate psychic attack and to assist earthbound spirits to leave an area.

COPPER: provides a harmonic connection between the physical and astral bodies and aligns the subtle bodies. Activates and conducts electrical impulses and can magnify energy from a healer or during rituals.

GARNET: seen as a sacred stone by Native Americans, Native South Americans and African tribal elders, it transforms energy and produces expansive awareness and vision. A stone for health and protecting your well-being. Provides purification, cleansing and elimination of what is in disorder in your body, mind and spirit.

BLOODSTONE: a stone that aligns the energy of the chakras, protects the astral body and balances the physical, emotional and intellectual bodies.

OBSIDIAN: this lustrous volcanic glass is an excellent grounding stone and provides a connection from the base of the spine into the earth. One of the best protective stones, it stabilizes your energy, provides a shield against negativity and transforms negative vibrations within the environment. Wearing it can disperse negative thoughts and protect you from those of other people.

PERIDOT: cleanses and stimulates the heart and solar plexus, regulates cycles and creates a shield of protection around the body. Peridot emits a warm, friendly energy.

HEMATITE: a stone for the mind, it protects against mental impurity and keeps you grounded.

TOURMALINE: relates to each of the chakras and acts to clear, maintain and stimulate each of the energy centres of the body. It has inherent electrical emanations which are revered throughout the world. It is used by shamans and priests as it brings healing powers to the user and provides protection from all dangers – physical and spiritual. Tourmaline wands are quite special and used for protecting the energy of a place or property.

JET: used to dispel fearful thoughts and can be used as protection against illness and violence. It is excellent as a protective stone for work and business.

IRON PYRITE: protects against deception and misunderstanding, and is useful when wanting to disappear for a time, or for protection in business ventures and new projects. Use carefully.

Wearing Crystals

Wearing crystals and minerals can have many positive effects – mental, emotional, physical and spiritual. Crystals respond, amplify and transmit at a very high level of vibrational frequency and have the ability to open us to other levels of awareness. They affect the aura, the energy field around us that contains within it the pattern of our lives, thoughts and emotions.

You can wear your crystal around your neck as a pendant with a gold or silver chain, or a cotton or leather thread. Generally the pendant should hang just above the sternum in the

centre of your chest, giving protection and energy to your heart chakra and throat area. The point of the crystal is generally placed downwards towards the magnetic pull of the earth. You can also carry your crystal in a cotton, leather or silk pouch, in your pocket or handbag.

All crystals pulse a powerful energy. The most powerful are the double terminated crystals, which have a point at both ends: these have not been cut or faceted in this way, but are natural. A single terminated crystal has a single point at one end and is often uneven at the other, where it was broken off from its foundation.

A double terminated crystal contains within it the two opposites of negative and positive, female and male, and if you wear or carry one it will stimulate your energy to help explore the extremes in yourself. This is not always comfortable but they do bring you back to a point of balance. They also help with receiving and giving energy and are powerful communicator crystals. However, if you are new to crystals I recommend that you work with a single terminated one until you understand the power of crystals and are aware of your day-to-day moods and how your life affects your inner world.

When choosing a crystal to wear it is best to wear clear quartz until you get to know your own energy then choose other types of crystals such as tourmaline for protection or amber for power, etc. My favourite is rose quartz, which gives off a loving energy that reminds me to be gentle and caring – particularly to myself.

Choosing Crystals

When choosing crystals always trust your gut instincts. Feel and touch them, experiment with different stones to find out the best type for your personality and home. If you are choosing a crystal for the first time, try not to let the logical part of your mind make the decision. Crystals speak through feeling and intuition – trust your feelings and you will choose the right one for you.

The most successful way to get the feel of a stone is to pick it up in your right hand and hold it near the centre of your chest around the level of your heart. Hold it for a few minutes, rotating it so that each side of the crystal is near, though not touching, your chest. You may get a sensation of coolness or warmth, your heart might flutter or quicken its beat, the hairs on your arm may stand on end, or you may just experience a deep connection with the stone and know that it's the right one. A heavy feeling in your chest, or one of irritation or coldness,

may suggest that the stone is not suitable for you or that crystal has been damaged in some way since it was taken from its place of origin.

Choosing Crystals to Enhance Your Sacred Space

Crystals are natural objects essential to successful sacred space. To choose crystals for your home you need to decide which room needs which particular type of crystal. This largely depends on the activities that take place there and the personalities of the people who use the room. At home, for instance, we have rose quartz (which gives off a gentle peaceful loving energy) in our bedroom, and amethyst and natural quartz (which enhance the atmosphere, giving it a sense of clarity and focus) in our living room. In each room place the crystal either on a table or in the four corners of the room, or hang it on the windowsill – anywhere where it is safe yet can send its vibrational frequency into the atmosphere.

And don't neglect the garden – crystals can also be used outdoors.

Ways to Honour Your Crystals

Crystals are a bit like pets – the better you look after them the more responsive they will be. Here are a few tips for looking after your charges.

- Smudge them regularly with sage bundles.
- Cleanse your crystals regularly by submerging them for 36– 70 hours in a solution of pure seawater or a sea salt solution. Do this once a month or, if you are using your crystals to work with a lot of people, weekly.
- Handle them carefully, lovingly and respectfully as they are living souls.
- Once a month let them sit in the light of the full moon.
- Place them on an altar in a natural setting, then sing, pray or chant for them to give them power and energy. Sunset or sunrise is a good time to do this.
- Give them offerings of incense, and light candles close by them on the altar – again this gives them energy.
- Once a month, after washing them, you can bury them in soft soil – preferably in your garden. The best position is by a tree close to the roots or, if you don't have a garden, in a plant pot on a windowsill so the moonlight and the night air touches its energy. This gives the crystal earth energy and grounds its power.

Using Crystals in Daily Life

Once you have acquired and cleaned your crystal you will need to get to know it. You do this simply by spending time with it, feeling it, holding it, wearing it and carrying it. The more time you spend with your crystal the greater your communication and rapport with it will be. Tune into your crystal by holding it in the right hand and touch the point to the palm of the left hand. Then rotate the crystal clockwise until you feel a tightening – this is aligning your energy to its vibration. Listen as well (this will help with your psychic skills), as crystals do actually sing! It is their method of communication and it will teach you to communicate telepathically.

When you're holding a crystal during meditation or healing it should point heavenwards to bring the light down. Don't overuse your crystal. By wearing them or carrying them too often you can leave them drained, so once a month honour or cleanse your working crystals. The ones placed around your home should be checked every few weeks to see if they want to be moved or cleaned.

The crystal you place on your altar is your sacred crystal so it needs be ritualized before being placed. This harmonizes their vibration to the frequency of your divine energy.

Making Your Crystal Sacred

First cleanse it in salt water for 24 hours, then bury it in the earth for another 24 hours. Now place it on the windowsill so it is filled with sunlight and moonlight for 24 hours. When you have completed the cleansing cycle, place the crystal on your sacred space and give thanks to the spirit within the crystal for coming into your life. Place a few pieces of natural herbs such as sage or sweet grass, or herbs from your garden, around the crystal as a gift, then burn incense and pass the crystal through the smoke, letting the fragrance cover every part. Wrap the crystal up in a soft, dark cloth and keep it covered from full moon to full moon. During this time every night hold it near your heart still wrapped in the cloth and communicate to the crystal your love, energy and prayer for a few minutes. When the month is over, unwrap the crystal and place it in the centre of your altar to represent the heart or centre of your sacred space.

Programming Your Tools

To be able to use a tool for psychic or spiritual work you have to programme the tool to work for you. This is first achieved by channelling its particular properties towards what you want from it. If you are programming a crystal, you have to be clear and simple. For instance, to programme a crystal to protect your emotions from negative energy, hold the chosen crystal in the palm of your hand and close your eyes. Relax your body and try to clear your mind of any mundane thoughts. Breathe and relax. Focus on your breathing and with every breath you will feel calmer and more relaxed. Now ask the crystal to use its power to guide and protect you. Imagine a waterfall of light washing over you, hold the terminated end of the crystal to your solar plexus (emotional body) and imagine yourself becoming very calm and strong like a tree with its roots deep in the earth. See yourself being confident and calm when you are dealing with people or situations that can make you feel unsafe or unprotected. Visualize these thoughts flowing into and remaining in the crystal. Carry the crystal with you when you need protection and know that it will project back to you your programmed thoughts.

Crystal Meditation

This meditation takes about an hour and should be done in your sacred space (see section 7). It helps ground and reconnect your spirit to your body.

- Select four of your favourite crystals. To prepare, burn some incense and light a candle. Now sit quietly, breathe deeply and enter a meditative state. You will be lying down for this meditation, so you need to place a crystal next to where your feet and each of your hands will be. The last crystal should be placed just above the crown of your head. Lay down, pick up the crystals and begin to breathe and relax. Call upon the powers of the earth to connect with your crystals and ask the great mother for healing, peace and relaxation.

- Now imagine that a beam of light comes out of the centre of your back, up from within the earth, and enters each crystal. See each crystal beginning to vibrate with light and begin to energize your body, entering from your feet up through your legs into the centre of your body, then spreading down your arms into your hands and connecting with the crystals in your hands. The power of light then moves up into your chest and connects with your heart, then moves up towards the crystal at your crown. Once you feel that each crystal is interconnected with light and with your physical body, allow yourself to drift off into a state of relaxation – even if your mind is chattering away your body will feel the healing powers from each crystal.

- Visualize yourself in an isolated forest and in the centre there is a huge oak tree with its branches reaching to the sky, gently moving from side to side. See your four crystals at the bottom of the tree and imagine that you pick up each stone and place it around your body. Then imagine that

you are being held within the branches of the tree and gently rocked until your body feels part of the tree. Feel a green light come up through the tree into your body, beginning at your feet and gently moving through each cell, each fibre, each organ, muscle and nerve end until your body feels completely healed by the green light. Then, as the healing is complete, sense yourself dropping down from the tree back onto the earth and journey back down into your body. You can play soothing music or be in complete silence, whatever suits you best.

- When you have completed the meditation, journey down from the crown crystal back through your heart taking the energy back into your hands and down your body into your feet. Then feel the earth crystal by your feet draw from your body all your tiredness and pain into the earth.

- Before you get up wiggle your toes, open your eyes, clench your fists and breathe deeply. Get up by bending your knees to your chest, turning over to your left and kneeling down on the floor with your hands supporting your body – then stand up.

You can also do this mediation by just placing a crystal on your heart chakra and feeling the energy moving outward from the centre of your body.

Crystals and Dreaming

For this exercise you need incense, candles, crystals, a note pad and pen. This is a powerful process so only do it if you feel ready to open up to your psychic energy centres. Don't underestimate the power of the crystals as the effect on your sleep state is profound.

- Smudge yourself and the room that you sleep in (see page 149).

- Choose stones that correspond with the energy, healing or transformation you would like to work with on a subconscious level.

- Smudge the stones, then say a prayer inviting their powers and guidance from the divine universe/God.

- Place them around your bed, underneath your bed or under your pillow.

- Place a notebook and pen by your bed and immediately on waking write down whatever comes to you or whatever you can remember of your dreams.

- The stone kingdom will continue to connect and energize you after you awaken, so be aware of any subtle or obvious sign. This exercise activates your openness to psychic energy.

- Repeat this process until you feel there is a strong and open line of communication and receptivity between you and the psychic world.

You can programme crystals for many types of tasks: for healing, for psychic intuition, for protection or sacred rituals and so on. You can also give programmed crystals as gifts for family and friends. We have chosen certain crystal pendants for our children and for our close friends, choosing specific types according to what kind of physical or emotional energy the crystal emits and what the recipient needs.

Programming Your Crystals for Psychic Vision

During my psychic development course one of my favourite workshops was working with crystals. The aim was primarily to open our psychic vision to enable us to see through the crystal into the future, but also to encourage a natural healing ability by working with stones.

The workshop meditation consisted of us holding a natural quartz crystal in the palm of our hands while the teacher talked us into a meditative state and we began to journey through the centre of the stone into the spirit world of crystals. I used to take off into the inner realms, journeying through underground passages until I reached a place of great beauty reflected by thousands of crystals and precious stones. In the centre was a beautiful old woman whom I sat beside and asked for guidance. I began to see images, symbols and hazy images of people and situations. I could remember many of the images and relayed them to the group: in some cases the images were relevant to the people sitting in the class, other times the images were pertinent to my life and family.

As I became confident with this technique I began to use it for psychometric readings. I asked clients to first hold the crystal in their hands for about 10 minutes, touching and rolling the crystal around so their energy would connect with it. I then took the crystal back and held it until I began to see images and symbols relevant to the client.

To programme your crystal for psychic readings, hold the crystal and call upon the powers of vision to be bestowed into the crystal. Crystals enhance the power of vision but you have to first work with a crystal for a while to know whether the psychic impressions are coming easily. If they are not, then perhaps you have chosen the wrong crystal for this work.

Crystal balls are also used for scrying or crystal gazing. They are used for divination – as a focus to attract the attention of the psychic gazer. The points of light reflected from the polished surface help to fix the eye until the optic nerve becomes fatigued and stops transmitting to the brain. This slows the brain waves down and you can then begin to see images and

visions with the inner eye rather than the outer. Crystal gazing has been practised since Egyptian times and is still very popular for fortune telling.

If you are going to work with crystals for divination purposes or for healing it is useful to have more than one. In addition, it is a good idea to separate the ones that are for you personally from those you use for working with others. I do not let anyone touch my personal crystals, yet my working crystals enjoy the challenge of working with so many contrasting frequencies.

Dowsing

The art of dowsing has been in existence for thousands of years. The ancient Chinese and Egyptians, for instance, are known to have practised it. Today, all over the world, there are many thousands of dowsers taught by various schools of thought. Practitioners such as Tom Graves have inspired many to learn the skill of detecting ley lines and energy fields within the earth, and not just that of water divining. In the last century finding water sources was the dowsers' main focus, while today dowsers can be called in to find the subtle electromagnetic fields emanating from underground streams, oil, ley lines, minerals – even dead bodies.

Dowsing is one the best ways to use your intuition to tune into your living spaces. Rod dowsing is commonly used in feng shui practice to detect underground water, geomagnetic lines, ley lines or earth grid lines – all of which affect the energy of a home or garden.

Anyone can dowse – it's just a skill that requires practice. First you need a dowsing, or divining instrument and some idea of what to do with it. Dowsing instruments can be divided into three different groups:

- angle rods made of metal
- hazel or spring rods
- pendulums

Dowsing instruments are simply amplifiers of movements often too small to be seen or felt. Most dowsing reactions show themselves as small movements of the hands so dowsers use instruments to make these movements more obvious.

The pendulum is the most versatile of all instruments, but it is the most susceptible to psychological interference; while in the natural wilds of the countryside nothing beats using a spring rod. It is better therefore to learn about all three types of dowsing instrument so you can choose the right tool for each job.

Rod Dowsing

There are two types of dowsing rod – the angle rod and the spring rod. The angle rod can be made of any kind of metal, from coat hangers to welding rods, and consists of two L-shaped rods. The short arm of each rod is the part that you hold. The idea is that the rods can swing freely from side to side so you must be relaxed when you hold them. Hold the rods in lightly clenched fists, roughly horizontal at the level of your solar plexus, keeping your wrists well apart, say about body width, and make sure that you don't bring your elbows in towards your body as this will make you feel cramped. The rods should be pointing away from you and roughly parallel to each other. This is what dowsers call their working or 'neutral' position. When working the angle rods the most common movements are inwards and outwards or up and down. The angle rods are not the easiest dowsing instruments to use and can be quite draining if you are working with them for a long period of time.

The spring rod, which is usually a Y-shaped rod, is sometimes made from a twig cut out of the hedgerow or two strips of springy material fastened together. When using a Y-shaped rod the idea is to hold it so its natural springiness gives it a highly unstable balance. You hold the rod by its two short ends, one in each hand. Hold these loosely in your fists so that nothing prevents them from swinging freely. Keep the palms horizontal and facing up, or horizontal and facing down. When the dowsing rod picks up energies emanating from the earth, it will swing in the direction of the energy flow.

Pendulum Dowsing

Not everyone finds the rods easy to use, and the pendulum is an excellent alternative. It is the easiest form of dowsing and is especially useful for detecting energy – whether home energy fields or personal energy. I would highly recommend you learn to use it, not only for asking questions but also to help with psychic energy and healing.

A pendulum is any weight – usually a crystal, stone or wooden or metal bob – connected to the end of a cord or chain. The choice of a bob is personal taste. However, from a point of view of inertia and balance, a bob should be reasonably symmetrical around its axis and

shouldn't be too long or else it will tend to wobble rather than swing. You can make your own pendulum but it is just as easy to buy a ready-made one from a crystal shop. Buy one that feels good and that you enjoy touching and holding.

Before you begin to work with your pendulum, you will need to energize it. Do this by holding it in your hand and imagining light coming out of your heart through the inside of your arms into the palms of your hands, so that energy is coming from you into the pendulum. Energizing or programming your pendulum and connecting with it enables it to work for you in an accurate way.

Using a Pendulum

Sit or stand in a relaxed fashion, with your shoulders back and your arms at right angles to your body. Hold the cord of the pendulum between the first finger and thumb of either hand, leaving about three to twelve inches of cord between your fingers and the bob or crystal, so it can swing freely and smoothly. Gently press your elbows against your body to help steady you and ground your energy. Now swing the pendulum gently back and forth, resting your mind on its oscillation so that its line of swing, its axis of swing, remains stable. There are two kinds of reaction: a change from oscillation to gyration, either clockwise or anti-clockwise; and a change in the axis of swing. The pendulum is harder to use when walking, so if you must move do so carefully as your movement will affect how the pendulum reacts.

When working with the pendulum your need to get accustomed to using it. Ask it a question to which you already know the answer. This will help you decipher the movements and interpretations. What does it do when indicating a yes or no? Also, each pendulum is different so never assume that if one pendulum goes clockwise for yes it would be the same for another pendulum. They are all individual so you need to work with them to get to know their rhythms.

Some people believe that we can interfere with the interpretation of the pendulum when working with them in this personal way. The three most obvious forms of 'psychological meddling', as Tom Graves calls it, are:

- attempting to control consciously the automatic part of the dowsing process
- the intrusion of conscious and semi-conscious assumptions and prejudices, and the problem of keeping your mind on what you are supposed to be doing
- unconscious assumptions and prejudices

You can overcome the first two consciously but the last one is a part of spiritual awareness and the recognition of knowing yourself well enough to recognize your resistances.

When asking a pendulum a question there are two simple ways of ensuring that you don't get it wrong. The first is to ask it if you can ask that question, i.e. whether or not you have the prerequisite knowledge necessary for receiving the answer you seek. For example, if you are asking about energy lines in your home and you don't really know what energy lines are, the pendulum will not be able to answer your questions because of your limited knowledge – so stick to what you know about.

The next consideration is *should* you know the answer to the question? By this I mean is it in your best interest to receive knowledge about an issue at this particular time. Sometimes we are not ready to receive the answers to our questions – this also applies when we use tarot cards or oracle cards to interpret questions or divine the future.

The key is to remember to ask simple, clear questions – the way you frame your question will determine how accurate and useful the information you receive will be.

It is best to work when you are feeling relaxed and not anxious or in a hurry (if you are anxious or nervous the pendulum may 'freeze'). Quieten your thoughts and access your intuitive self; breathe, relax and just enjoy working with your pendulum. Dowsing is not an act to be forced or controlled. You are a channel and sometimes the answers or the movement flows easily, sometimes it does not. The key is to enjoy and relax.

When working with dowsing instruments sometimes you need to know more than just a yes or no answer, for instance if you need to investigate a fault line within the energy in your home. In such cases you need to work out the degree of information that you need, the degree of rightness or wrongness, the density of problem, or depth of water etc.

Interpretation of Messages

There are two kinds of interpretation: one analytical and the other intuitive. The analytic kind is based on repeatability; if a dowsing reaction is repeated under the same conditions it is held 'true' and the meaning of that reaction is derived from the conditions under which it took place. For example, if a reaction is happening over the same spot in your home or garden every time you walk over that spot with the same instruments and in the same conditions, then there is something causing the reactions at that spot. You then begin to investigate what it could be, building up a picture of whatever it is you're looking for – its position, size, depth, composition and qualities.

The intuitive interpretation is based on the belief that dowsing works because we subconsciously tune into the stream of wisdom accessible at the level of the collective unconscious. This is a place in the mind that is able to interpret information that is on a subliminal or subtle level. The dowser receives information from this source, causing muscles to twitch and react, which in turn causes the rod to turn or a pendulum to swing. The body of the dowser becomes a part of the instrument of dowsing; it is the radio station that receives the waves of information from the energy flows within the earth. The tool acts like an amplifier for the information received and the clearer the belief or faith in dowsing the more powerful the messages received. This is similar to being a clairvoyant who is able to receive messages from the spirit world – the more confident the medium, the clearer the messages. The intuitive interpretation is based on the inherent meaning, a sense of 'rightness' or 'wrongness' transmitted through the dowsing instrument.

Body Reactions

There are many 'body reactions' you can use as signals when dowsing. Most dowsers learn to use hand reflexes but other signals include momentary stomach ache, a loss of balance, a tightening of the back or neck muscles, a tic of the eyelids, a yawn – even a sequence of hiccups or burps. Anyone can train themselves to react to the experience of dowsing. This is done by learning how your body as a whole reacts during a dowsing operation.

'When dowsing you must be aware that there are some dangers in working with this method of tuning into the earth and its inner kingdoms. We may be delving into places which our ancestors called the kingdoms of the gods, and world mythologies and religions term the underworld. It is therefore vital that you do not delve where angels fear to tread – unless you are fully conversant with psychic protection and the guardianship of your spiritual energy.

'In the early stages of developing your skill, it is important to be guided by your instincts – if you feel afraid, stop working with your tool/pendulum and close off your energy from the work that you are doing. Go home, have a bath in sea salt to cleanse your energy, and monitor how you are feeling over a 24-hour period. If you are still feeling nervous or insecure or exhausted you must seek a good healer to have your aura cleansed (you also need to bury your dowsing tool in the earth for 24 hours to cleanse it). It may be that the area you are working on has been disturbed by some ancient latent power – if you suspect this may be the case, call in a professional.'

Terry O'Sullivan, Soul Rescuer

Remember that your first response is best. When you have practised with questions to which you know the answers, progress to ones you don't know the answers to but can find out. When asking a new question, stop the instrument completely and start again. The more practice you have, the more accurate your ability will become and the more your confidence will increase. Once you have gained confidence about your dowsing abilities you can begin to apply this skill in your everyday life.

Do bear in mind, however, that dowsing is mentally very tiring. If you overuse the rods or pendulum you may find that you are beginning to feel tired, physically or mentally. If so, leave them for a couple of days and, if you're a beginner, only practise for half an hour at a time.

Dowsing your Home

Start in the garden. Walk along your garden in a straight line, up and down, plotting the responses from your rods (I find rods more useful when working in nature or in a property, and tend to use the pendulum for working on someone's body or energy). As you plot the reactions begin to search for clues to those reactions, such as underground water pipes, etc. Now walk around the outside of the house. Begin at the front and walk round clockwise (if you can), again plotting your findings on a map or drawing of the land. If you can, get a detailed map of your house, street and local area that shows waterways, electrical cable, etc. You can also use archivist records or older maps of the area to tell you what the land was once used for.

Be clear as to what you are programming the dowsing instrument to discover for you. For instance, if you are seeking water flow around or under the house it will pick only that information up. After you have dowsed around the house dowse again outside the edges of the house itself. Again mark on your map what you find. Finally, walk through the house from the front and around each room and mark the map accordingly. Compare the map of your findings outside the house with what you observed inside – and check whether any lines of energy cross the entire house.

When checking a house with the rods, note which room is creating the greatest disturbance and why. Is it because it is used as the family room with computers and TV? Or are there other influences? Use your intuition – objects and antiques can cause problems just as much as a property's history and background.

If you are going to use your rods or pendulum on a regular basis, I recommend that you read one of the many good books on the market (see Resources section, page 180).

Looking After your Dowsing Tools

Where should you keep them? I wrap my rods in a natural fibre cloth and keep them in a safe place or hang them in the window to receive the light of the sun and the moon. Crystal pendulums should be soaked in salted water once a month. It is also advisable to bury them in the earth for a month, once a year, for a complete cleanse. Pendulums also enjoy receiving the light from the sun and the moon so hang them on the windowsill when you are not using them.

Scent

Using Fragrance to Create a Sacred Atmosphere

Improving the quality of energy that surrounds you can be undertaken in many different ways. Each culture has its equivalent of blessing and making sacred a place or a home using rituals and ceremonies. It is entirely a matter of personal preference what you wish to do – how elaborate the rituals and what kind of scents you enjoy working with. I love burning fragrant incense, herbs or essential oils to make my home or workplace peaceful, healing and spiritual, and manage to fit in a weekly purification around the home using a sage bundle or a vapourizer with my favourite essential oil. It makes such a difference to the well-being of the home.

Here are some of the best methods of using fragrances.

Aromatherapy

This therapy uses the aromas of the plant kingdom – flowers, trees, herbs and bushes. The essences of these plants are put through a process – known as distillation – to extract the plant's essential oil. Essential oils are highly concentrated and should always be diluted before being used. Each fragrance evokes a different mood so they can be used to achieve different purposes such as soothing, uplifting, cleansing and healing.

Methods of Use

ATOMIZER

To invoke energy that is conducive to the positive emotions in your home, you might like to try combining aromatherapy with misting. Add just four drops of essential oil to your misting water. Don't use more than this, or you could clog up your spray. You can also make up a small atomizer bottle to use on yourself: fill it with spring water and a drop of your favourite aromatherapy fragrance and mist your body, starting from your head, across your face and neck area and down over your chest. Misting revitalizes your energy field and cleanses your aura.

NEUTRALIZING EMOTIONAL CHARGES

Emotional energy tends to stagnate in rooms after emotional events. After an argument the air in a room might seem thick, almost charged – and indeed it is, as there is an electric charge left hanging in the air as a residue from all the negative emotions. The fastest way to neutralize this residual energy is to mist the room using a spray with water and a purifying aromatherapy oil such as pine, eucalyptus, tea tree or cypress. Misting not only neutralizes emotional charges in a room almost instantly, it also creates a special negative-ion-rich environment similar to the energy you feel at a waterfall or by the sea.

To neutralize negative emotional charges, add four or more drops of your chosen oil to 300 ml/10 fl oz water, then walk around your room or space in a clockwise direction, spraying or flicking water as you go. If you come to a place in the room that feels exceedingly stagnant or 'sticky' then spray a little more there.

DIFFUSERS

These are specially made for use with essential oils. There are all sorts of diffusers – some heated by candle flame and others by electricity – but the important thing is that they heat the oil, so allowing its molecules to be released into the atmosphere.

The most popular choice is the ceramic vapourizer. This has a small bowl that sits on top of the unit holding the candle. The bowl is filled with water and a few drops of oil are added, the candle then heats this up, releasing a gentle flow of scent (use 1–6 drops to a small amount of water). When buying a ceramic vapourizer, ensure the surface of the bowl section is non-porous so it can be wiped clean and another essential oil used later.

You can also use special vapourizing ceramic rings or non-flammable rings which can be placed on light bulbs with a few drops of essence added to the rings. Make sure whatever method you use that you always place the burner in a safe place.

RADIATORS

Put 1–9 drops of essential oil on a cotton wool ball and lodge it by the pipe or somewhere where it is in contact with the heat.

WATER BOWLS

Put boiling water into a bowl and add 1–9 drops of your chosen essential oil. Close doors and windows and allow five minutes for the aroma to permeate the room.

WOOD FIRES

Use cypress, pine, sandalwood or cedarwood oils. Put 1 drop on each log and leave for half an hour before using, although oil will retain its effectiveness for a very long time so the logs can all be prepared in advance. One log per fire will be sufficient.

Choosing your Oils

More than any of our other senses, smell affects our emotional reaction to people and situations. It has been shown that the way someone smells will provoke a stronger reaction in others than the way they look or sound.

To discover what suits your personality – and that of your home – try out a variety of essential oils at different times of day, in different rooms. In the morning, you're more likely to need something uplifting, whereas in the afternoon or evening you may want a relaxing or calming essence. You can also use essences to lift depression, counter stress, ease fatigue and can help restore energy levels at work or at home during the day.

- Uplifting oils: rose, jasmine, neroli, ylang ylang, chamomile, roman or German chamomile
- Oils for fatigue and drained energy: rosemary, thyme, peppermint, rose, olibanum, jasmine, neroli, juniper
- To uplift and harmonize the atmosphere: rose, jasmine, mandarin, lime, lemongrass, orange, grapefruit
- For a relaxing atmosphere: lavender, chamomile, rose, geranium, cedarwood, clary sage
- To purify the atmosphere and cleanse your energy: peppermint, camphor, eucalyptus, thyme, rose, sage, cedarwood, pine, ginger, tea tree, rosemary, cypress
- To calm the atmosphere: myrrh, frankinsence, melissa, lavender, mandarin, bergamot, sandalwood, palma rosa, patchouli, petitgrain, rose absolute, vanilla absolute

Herbs

There are two methods of using herbs to cleanse your aura or space. One is by using herb bundles that you burn (smudging), the other is soaking herbs in water and using the water as a purifier.

In certain native traditions, the shaman dips the ends of branches or sprigs of plants into purified water and then flicks them around the room as part of a purification ritual. To cleanse a room using this method, begin by taking a small bowl of spring water and say a prayer over the water to ask your god/divine spirit to bless the cleansing ritual. Take your bowl of water to the centre of the room along with your chosen sprig or herb or plant, dip it into the water to soak for a moment, then flick the sprig into each corner and into the adjacent areas and say out loud or in a silent prayer, 'may the power of the herb (whatever you have chosen) and the power of the water cleanse and purify this sacred space, blessed be'. This helps with the spiritual intention of your action and allows divine intervention to cleanse the energy of your room.

Herbs to Cleanse and Uplift the Atmosphere

PINE: ideal for clearing heavily polluted energy. It is good in the bedroom after illness or when the atmosphere feels dead and lifeless.

CEDAR: this has similar properties to pine but is used more for cleansing emotional and spiritual energies.

SAGE: used by Native Americans for their sacred ceremonies and now popularized in Europe for space clearing rituals, meditation practice and preparing a room for psychic communication.

LEMON VERBENA: this is very good for stagnant energies or negative emotional energies such as anger and rage, as lemon verbena has invigorating and stimulating properties as well as a soothing energy.

ROSEMARY: an excellent fragrant herb which cleanses and uplifts the energy. It is very good if you have been feeling a little low or depressed.

And let's not forget flowers. They bring a lightness and gentleness into the room. Every flower has its own unique energy – my favourites are lilies, roses and daisies, as they give beauty, love and innocence.

Smudging

Smudging is the traditional Native American way of using smoke to purify a space. The smoke produced by the ritual burning of herbs is used to alter the energy of a specific space, oneself or another when conducting a ritual or ceremony in a sacred way.

Many herbs are used for a smudging ritual, the most common being sage and sweet grass or cedar. You can also use other herbs more easily obtained in your local area. Smudge sticks are also available from specialist shops including some health food shops, alternative bookshops and mind, body, spirit festivals. You can also make your own bundles for smudging, but it is essential to honour the plants that you pick at each step of the process as this makes the herb bundle more powerful. (See page 149 for how to smudge.)

Incense

The use of incense is widespread in much of the Far East and Asia, particularly in China, India and Nepal. In these countries people use incense to worship their gods and deities, to bless and purify their homes and at religious ceremonies. Incense purifies the energies of a place. This is not the same as space clearing, where the aim is to cleanse your space of negative energy. Instead, incense brings in a purity, a sacred or spiritual essence.

Purifying with Incense

Most people simply light the end of the incense stick, blow out the flame once it has taken and then leave it to smoulder. However, you can increase the purification power of incense by using the following technique.

- As you light the incense take a few seconds to say a prayer of dedication – this enhances the power of a sacred act.

- Once you have begun burning the stick, move around each room in your home or office in a clockwise direction, making circles with the incense around the doors and windows and the four corners of each room. This multiplies the purification power at these important entry points.

- Pay special attention to rooms that are important to you, such as your bedroom or work room. If there are bedrooms where sick members of your family are convalescing or one that is occupied continuously by clients or business meetings then spend an extra few minutes burning incense in that room.

- When you have finished purifying all the rooms, allow the incense to burn out. Do not empty the incense ash down the toilet or throw it in the bin, instead wrap it in a piece of paper and empty it into the earth in your garden or local park. As the burning of the incense was a sacred act so the power that has been called in needs to go back into the earth when you have completed the purification.

I like to light at candle at the end of this ritual to acknowledge the sacred essence and to bring a sense of peace into the atmosphere.

The quality of space purification depends on the quality of incense used. The incense used by the Chinese to make joss sticks is fine, and the best scent for this is sandalwood or a mixture of sandalwood with another incense. (I enjoy the scent of jasmine and rose which gives a more feminine atmosphere.) Incense from India and Nepal is stronger and more pungent and is usually too heavy for small spaces, but this is a personal thing so I recommend you try a variety before you decide what you like. The scents you use are very important. The energy changes from one situation to another, so you will need several varieties on hand to accommodate your changing needs.

Using Fragrance to Make Sacred Space

Fragrance can be used to create a sacred space for specific purposes or to create a certain atmosphere.

PEACE Use either one or all of the following: burn pure frankincense on a charcoal burner, light a blue candle, burn a sage and lavender herb bundle to smudge the space, use a few drops of sandalwood essential oil in a vapourizer.

PSYCHIC POWER Burn pure pine or sandalwood in a charcoal burner or as an essential oil in a atomizer before you begin working. For a more intense and powerful atmosphere try orange or lemongrass essential oils. Personally I like palma rosa or rosewood as they create a gentle atmosphere. When I need cleansing energy I use cypress or juniper.

EMOTIONAL UPLIFTMENT Use one or all of the following: burn cedarwood either in a charcoal burner or as a smudge stick; a few drops of lavender, cypress or pine in a vapourizer; burn pure rosemary in a charcoal burner.

SPIRITUAL INSPIRATION Use one or all of the following: burn an Indian or Tibetan incense stick, burn pure frankincense or myrrh on a charcoal burner, or add a few drops of chamomile roman, rose or jasmine to a vapourizer.

The Elements

The power of the elements are called upon in many circumstances as they bring in the physical essence of all of life, and they relate to us physically, emotionally and spiritually. The elements are the soil in which magic can manifest.

The powers of the elements play a part in both our internal and external world. For example, if we are too overbearing, if we have too much fire in our personality, then we may need to call on the essence of water to help us become more fluid and sensitive. If we need a better job we can call upon the element of air, of communication and connections to help. Before you can 'call upon the powers' you need to get to know the characteristics of the elements.

AIR may be described as the principle of movement. It cannot be seen, although its presence can be felt and observed by its effect on what it touches. Air is the element of freedom and spaciousness. It is light and expanding, therefore difficult to measure and contain. It represents the world of thoughts and a vision of the future.

FIRE may be described as the principle of expansion and transformation. Fire is associated with the sun, the ball of fire from which the entire solar system derives its light energy. Fire energy is expansive. Fire embodies passion, enthusiasm and desire. It is both light and heat. It represents the light of intelligence and the courage to follow it. It is the spark of passion and initiative.

WATER may be described as the principle of fluidity. Water flows and takes the shape of whatever contains it, and finds its own level. Water flows from the inside of rocks or pours gently from above, like feelings which 'well up' inside you or sweep over you. Tears, water flowing from the eyes are the outward expression of strong emotional essence. Water imbibes all life forms and gives them lushness and freshness. Without feelings, the soul would be an arid landscape of calculations, speculations and unresponsiveness.

EARTH may be described as the principle of inertia and stability. Earth is the taking of form, the appearance of solidity. Earth is the ground we step on; it is the mother and the home. It is the source and the provider for all physical needs. The element earth in the inner world represents sensations – good or bad, sensuous or isolated, at ease or uncomfortable. It represents where you come from and the natural instincts that guide you to food and shelter, to warmth and security.

The Elements and the Spirit Realms

The elements can be related to the four main planes of reality within the spirit world. Earth is related to the physical, the material plane of ordinary, everyday reality. It relates to the world of matter, which is perceived through the five physical senses of sight, hearing, touch, taste and smell. Water is related to the astral plane, the realm of desire whose reality is perceived through feelings and emotions. Air is related to the mental plane, the realm of thought and creativity whose reality is perceived through the mind. Fire is related to the spiritual plane, which is perceived through the heart. The spiritual plane is experienced through unconditional love. Only through giving itself can the isolated, individual self experience the being of another and by doing so experience the very essence of life itself.

The Psychological Properties of the Four Elements

The elements express themselves in the human personality in some of the following ways.

Air

Air is the great transforming element as it is in constant motion. So air-orientated people may find themselves moving from thing to thing, busying themselves in all sorts of activities, or perhaps only finding satisfaction when they have plenty to do. They need activity or they become bored.

An air person seeks expression through communication, by taking the imitative in communication, by putting into form what has already been established or by changing the methods of communication. Air stimulates – it is clear and uncluttered, it provides impetus, it is the aspect of thought, or intellect and will express itself in mental and verbal communication, in ideas, in social popularity. Air is yang as it is active and expansive.

Fire

Fire people will have a fiery enthusiasm for almost anything that captures their interest at a particular time, and may find a need to curb the tendency to be so all-consuming that they become possessive. They seek expression through ideas, by initiating new ideas, consolidating accepted ideas and by making changes to ideas to meet fresh circumstances.

Fire energizes, it ignites and consumes. Fire is the element of transmutation, it brings about dramatic changes. Fire is the realm of spirituality, of sexuality and passion. It expresses itself particularly in creativity, enthusiasm and drive, in extroverted behaviour and versatility. Fire is yang because it is active and penetrating.

Water

Water people are likely to be adaptable and easy going, and may find the necessity of fitting in with their surroundings and with others essential to their feeling at ease.

Water seeks expression through ideas, through formulating and establishing them or through modifying them to suit the changing times. Water dispenses, it is fluid and constantly changing. It is the element of absorption and germination. Water is the realm of love and the emotions. Water expresses itself particularly in imagination, sympathy and understanding, sensitivity, and introverted behaviour. Water is yin because it is receptive.

Earth

For earth people stability and security are essential. Earth seeks expression through work in three ways: through initiating work, through completing work or by changing the way work is done.

Earth contains, it is stable. Earth is the foundation of the elements and the one we are the most comfortable with because it is solid and dependable. Earth is the realm of abundance and prosperity. Earth expresses itself particularly in practicalities, patience and persistence, sensuality, conservatism and cautiousness. Earth is yin because it is fertile, nurturing and fruitful.

It is very likely that one of the elements will attract you more than the others; at the same time another one will feel uncomfortable to you. The reason is that hardly anybody is in perfect balance and it is normal to have too much of one element and too little of another. Feeling the various elements inside yourself, while you surround yourself physically with their symbols in your sacred space or on your altar can help re-establish the balance between them. The elements act like the poles on an electrical circuit and will make the energy field surrounding you stronger and healthier, giving you both increased well-being and an awareness of all your faculties.

Tune into the Elements Within

- Lie down in a comfortable position or sit in a chair and just relax the body. Begin to breathe deeply and as you exhale tell your body to relax and inhale. Call upon your soul and connect to the centre of your being. Just by asking to connect it will begin to happen.

- From the centre of your being imagine a circle or wheel. At each axis of the wheel/circle you will place the power of the element, for instance it is traditional in sun astrology to place the power of fire in the south aspect, then place the power of the water in the west aspect, the power of earth in the north and the power of air in the east. Once you have seen the wheel connected to the centre of your being, journey to each aspect and see yourself become that element. How do you feel as you enter inside that power – comfortable, empty, uncomfortable, full?

- When you have completed the cycle go back to the centre and meditate on bringing into balance the unbalanced aspect. For instance if it is water, imagine that the water in the axis is growing and becoming more powerful, or if it is earth see the earth aspect become full and strong.

When you have finished redressing the balance bless your centre and return out of your meditation/ visualization and open your eyes. Add ingredients of the elements to your altar to enhance the rebalancing within your self. If you need more water place a water feature on the altar, more fire, add a red candle and light it daily, more earth, place a bowl filled with earth or a stone, more air, add a picture of clouds or sky.

Practical Ways to Redress the Balance

Once you understand where your imbalances lie you begin to nurture those elements in which you are weakest.

AIR
This is the world of thoughts and words, so if you are lacking that element, dedicate some of your time to an abstract pursuit – go to art galleries, read books, be creative.

FIRE
Feel the heat and warmth of the sun. Make a fire, burn candles, be physical and passionate with people, hold hands and feel the warmth of another person.

WATER

Make yourself slow down and go for a walk outside in the early hours of the morning when the dew is still on the ground and the leaves of plants and flowers. Be gentle with yourself, have a candle-lit bath, go swimming and be emotional. Cry!

EARTH

Grounding is essential to feel secure and to be present. Do little things around the house, tend to the garden, watch your plants grow, play with your children, walk in nature and meditate outdoors.

Creating sacred space in the home

The idea of sacred space is probably as old as humanity itself because the search for the spirit has always included the idea that the natural world is filled with signs and symbols of the divine. Sacred space is a physical expression of the divine or supernatural; a place where they can be experienced, where we can get in touch with that which is beyond the identity of ourselves and physical reality. The weaving of sacred space in your home creates a connection that will deepen your sense of relationship to all things: it symbolically expresses your connection to a divine source which, in turn, expresses its power, love and wisdom through you and in your life.

A sacred space in the home isn't in itself sacred; it works by showing us what has been there all along. It releases energy within us and around us that we simply may not have been aware of. As part of a creative process, it can help us refocus our spiritual vision.

A Home For the Soul

The very act of creating sacred space makes us spiritually receptive to the sacred – as well as giving us a physical place to pray, meditate and perform rituals. Rediscovering the importance of sacred space in our lives can take many different forms; there is no 'right' way of creating sacred space or using it. In addition to (or as part of) sacred space, many people create a family altar with photographs of all the members of the family and everyone who plays an important role in their life. This can help integrate our spiritual lives with our 'daily' lives.

The soul dwells in the world of spirits and is a part of your unconscious; it is powerfully affected by symbols so the expression of creativity in constructing a sacred space in your home is an expression of your soul. My sacred space (which I have transformed into a family altar) is a Welsh dresser inherited with the house. We fill each shelf with all our most treasured possessions – not the objects that have cost a great deal of money but the ones that are most important to our heart, to our love of life. The top shelf represents our relationship with our spiritual beliefs; and is home to an antique Tibetan necklace, an African bushman sculpture and a ceramic Madonna and child. On the lower shelves we have placed pictures of our children and a set of Victorian plates given to me by my grandmother. The drawers are filled with treasures we have found in nature – rocks, stones, shells, feathers, etc. It is chaotic and vibrant. It has all the visual clues about our lives as a family; it centres me and brings me back to what is important about my life.

For many people, reclaiming part of where they live as a sacred space is the first step in recovering a primordial sense of spirit. Whether you decide to make your altar or your room a reminder of the role spirit plays in your life, a place of meditation and prayer, or a focal point for ritual and ceremony is less important. What is vital is the intention to find that sacredness within and make it manifest without.

Before you think about creating a home for the soul you need to spend time getting to know the spirit of your home. The following exercise will help you understand your home and what is required to turn it into space that nourishes your soul.

Tuning into Your Home

- Close your eyes and allow yourself to relax. Go into your favourite room, turn down the lights and lie down. Take a few deep breaths and with each inhalation ask your spirit guides to give you the vision to see into your home. With each exhalation allow yourself to enter into a peaceful state of mind. Try to let go of your expectations of your home. Let the home show you its soul.

- Visualize yourself travelling to different parts of your home. Begin by approaching the front of the building. As you move through the front garden, what do you feel about the space? What colours and textures touch you? Do you like the feeling? If not, why?

- As you stand before the front part of your home ask your guardian spirit to show you the soul of your building. What feeling does it give you? Does it make you feel safe? Or does it make you afraid? What does it look like? For some people it may look like a person, or a tall elemental being, or an animal, it may be like an unseen presence, a voice, a light … or energy.

- Ask your spirit guardian to communicate with the soul of your home and ask it if you and your family are welcomed? Be true to the answer that you get. If it is yes then that is fine – acknowledge that you are welcomed and ask the soul of your home how you can best benefit from your relationship with it. Ask where you should build your sacred altar to celebrate your sacred space, as you will need to welcome the essence of your home into that space. If you have a garden, ask where within it you should you build a shrine to the spirits of nature.

- If the answer is no that you are not welcomed, you will either be aware that you are unhappy about where you are living or that you need to improve your spiritual relationship within your home.

- If you are aware that you should not be in this house as it is not conducive to your energy then it is time to work out a plan to move away. But before you do this, sort out where you want to go and when. (This you can also ask your spirit guardian and if the answer comes back very clear and simple then you can make some steps forward; if not then you still have lessons to learn from your experiences within this home.)

- If the soul of the home wishes you to improve your relationship with the sacred energy of the home then it is time to consider what needs to change within the structure of your personal relationship with yourself and others around you. As they say, your home is not just your castle, it is a reflection of your personality. Whether you are tidy or untidy is unimportant, it is whether you can live with yourself that matters.

- Imagine that you could make your home perfect for your soul. What kind of walls would it have, texture, colour … What kind of flooring, a real fire, candlelight?

- Go through your home room by room. As you enter each room how does it make you feel, what do you sense in that room, which ones make you happy, which ones feel sad or negative in any way? Try to remember your impressions so you can write them down when you come out of your meditation. What sounds, lighting, smells, colours and textures does each room have? As you are being lead ask your guardian spirit which rooms in the house need to be harmonized or cleansed. Which rooms are perfect for creating a sacred space for practising meditation and psychic awareness?

- Now journey into the room which is suitable for your sacred space and ask which part of the room would be ideal to build your altar.

- Go through your home room by room and imagine if you could change things around to suit the harmony of the sacred space of your home, what you would do. Move things around and keep going until your house is bright and positive and feels like the perfect home.

Once you have completed this exercise, recall what you experienced and write it down. Make your description as detailed as possible. In the coming days you can continue to add to your list.

When you have crystallized your thoughts about the perfect home for your soul, find a word that describes the feeling of this special place for you. For instance, one of my clients, a journalist, describes her sacred space as freedom. Her soul needs to feel space and liberation when she is at home, so to bring this current feeling into her home, we connected with her guardian spirit for inspiration. We were shown a time when she was very young and lived in South Africa. She realized it was the space and freedom of being brought up with so much nature around her that was missing from her very urban lifestyle. Her lounge was chosen as her sacred room. She moved out all the clutter (this is vital as it leaves space for new things and creates a sense of peace and calm in your home), took out one of three settees to free up the room, painted the walls, replaced the carpet with floorboards and an ethnic rug and introduced some of her favourite pieces from South Africa. And at the centre of the room there are always fresh flowers to say thank you to the earth mother. Now when she comes home in the evening she is able to walk into her lounge and feel liberated from the pressures of her daily life.

The Sanctuary – Your Sacred Room

The words 'sanctuary' and 'sanctify' come from the Latin *Sanctus* meaning holy or whole. Sanctifying a particular place implies making it holy, in this case making a place where you can experience wholeness or fullness of yourself, a place to go every day to connect, to touch base. Some sort of sanctuary is essential for the practice of psychic and spiritual techniques. Not all of us, however, have the luxury of being able to use somewhere like the lounge. For those of us with a family it is essential to choose a room that is away from the hustle and bustle of family life or your relationship. If you don't have the space to have a room for this practice then choose a corner of your bedroom where you can set up an altar and where you can meditate and take time out.

Once we have created your sacred space it is important that it is maintained in a way that will keep you connected with your sacred observances. Create the right kind of atmosphere by burning incense or essential oils – and use candlelight. When you light the candles affirm that you are creating this space with love and respect and ask the light to bless your space and make you feel safe and calm.

As well as making our homes conducive to our energies, we must also consider our workspace. Many of us spend a great deal of time at work yet often we neglect to make this space a reflection of our needs, wants and aspirations. Here, Davina MacKail – whose business experience combined with her understanding of feng shui, space clearing and psychic studies makes her an ideal contributor – shares her tips for creating sacred space within the workplace.

Creating a Sacred Space in the Workplace

In order to create a sacred space in the workplace we must be aware of our personal energy rhythms and how these affect the rise and fall of energy at different times of the day. We must also be able to communicate with work colleagues and clients in an intuitive and secure way that enhances our self awareness and confidence. Utilizing our psychic powers to foster harmonious relationships both with our own energies and those of our colleagues is essential to a successful working life, but so too are our surroundings. Look at your office – both the individual elements and its overall feel – with fresh eyes.

IMAGES AND SYMBOLS: Symbolism and imagery hold vital clues to our inner world. What metaphors can you read in your choice of artworks and photographs? Are they vibrant and alive or dark and dank? Do they make you feel good? If they represent your current life and you're happy with that, great – if they don't change them for something that supports your vision of the future.

YOUR DESK: If you can choose the placement of your desk try to ensure it is in a position that allows you to see whoever enters. This is called the command position and puts you in control of the room. With your back to the door, you will feel an unconscious vulnerability which can drain your energy and lead to feelings of anxiety. To cultivate a sense of being supported by your workplace sit with your back against a good solid wall. If that's not possible create the same sense of security using a bookcase or similar item of furniture, or ensure you have a high-backed executive-type chair.

YOUR CHAIR: Your office chair is the uniform you wear every day. Never scrimp in this area. It is what connects you to the earth, your personal source of energy. Your legs need to be at 90-degree angle with feet firmly planted on the floor. Use foot rests if necessary to ensure feet do not swing freely. Have lumber support and the ability to stretch out. Chairs should have a five-spoke base to ensure balance and solidity, with adjustable height, pelvic tilt and arm rests.

LIGHTING: People are healthier, happier and more productive in workplaces with good natural light. Windowless offices are stagnant and far harder to work in. Introduce your office to daylight bulbs and lamps and always use desk lamps, spots or up-lighters rather than neon overhead strip lighting which sucks positive energy out of a space and creates unnecessary heaviness for the souls who work beneath it.

CLUTTER: This is the biggest enemy of sacred space. If your office and desk is free of superfluous items, energy can freely flow around you. You will feel lighter and more in control. The space created allows you to hear your inner voice. Be ruthless with filing. Clear your in-tray daily. The higher the pile, the more you will feel stressed and overwhelmed, especially in these days of information overload. This applies equally to your computer. The work-tool of choice for most of us and just as prone to attracting junk! If business is slow, ruthless filing creates more space for new clients.

BRING NATURE INSIDE: Create a sense of vitality and connection by bringing the natural world inside. It will improve your health too. Real plants and fresh flowers absorb the harmful electromagnetic fields of office equipment and replace them with stimulating, positive vibes. Spider plants and peace lilies

are particularly effective. Beware of cacti and spiky leaves in confined areas as they can create an atmosphere for correspondingly sharp aggressive relationships. Money plants are great for enhancing prosperity. A vase of white flowers helps focus your attention when important tasks need attention.

CRYSTALS: Natural amethyst and rose quartz crystals cure negative computer emissions when placed close by. The manufactured, clear-faceted ones are exceptionally potent in activating the flow of positive energy. These can be used to enhance certain areas of your personal space. Use your intuition for placement. Make sure the crystals are cleansed regularly and programmed with your intention and the job you wish them to do. (It is also advisable to wipe your screen and keyboard with a damp cloth each morning to neutralize harmful ion emissions.)

FURNITURE: There are no straight lines in nature. Consequently, it creates a more positive flow of 'chi' if you avoid too many sharp corners from furniture and shelving when planning your office decor. Curves and round-edged designs are preferable for creative work. However, if the accounts need sorting or if there's a deadline looming a square desk will support the analytic skills and decisiveness required to complete these tasks.

As well as taking care of the practical elements of your workplace you should also examine how you take care of yourself whilst you are at work.

RELAXATION AT THE WORKPLACE: In the sacred office create the time to cultivate stillness. Take 5 minutes out of every hour to just 'be'. Usefulness emanates from space. Stillness lies behind all action. Image precedes matter.

GO OUT FOR LUNCH: Start your own personal campaign to bring back the lunch hour and get out of the office at least once during the day. Claim back your right for a midday nature fix and go for a walk in a nearby park or, if that's not possible, find a space outside to sit and visualize yourself in your favourite park, sitting under your favourite tree.

DIFFICULT PEOPLE: If you are faced with an angry client or colleague at work don't react defensively, however unprovoked their attack. Instead try changing your attitude. Send out positive vibrations and light from your heart centre to the person in question. I have suggested this to many clients with some extraordinarily positive results. Try it yourself for a week with every potentially confrontational situation you encounter. My guess is you'll want to extend the trial.

MEETINGS: Before a meeting spend time focusing on and writing down your personal intentions for the outcome. Then make a commitment to not be attached to the way your desired results manifest themselves. Clear the space using visualization techniques. If short of time just imagine clear white light filling the space and seal it by setting the whole room in an energetic bubble. Ask for whatever transpires during the meeting to be for the highest good of all involved. If you are running the event take a command position in the room, i.e. one that gives you a full view of the room and in particular the door so that you can see people entering and leaving. This enables you to feel secure. Practise a few minutes of grounding and deep breathing exercises before the meeting starts and trust the process.

A Home Altar

A home altar can act as a personal place of prayer, ritual and meditation and is one way of acknowledging the sacredness of all the space we inhabit. It serves as a kind of reminder of our connection to spiritual realms. The influence that your altar can have on your life is considerable because it is a visible expression of your spiritual life; it strengthens your connection with your past and future.

A home altar serves three main spiritual purposes: it can be used as a place to pray and ask for divine guidance; a place to listen to messages from the spirit realms; and somewhere to give thanks for blessings received and to celebrate the powers that guide you.

- **PRAYER AND DEVOTION:** Using a home altar for prayers can help instill a feeling that we are not alone – it functions as a reminder that there are beings in the spirit realms that are looking after us. This can provide the courage we need to face difficult obstacles.
- **LISTENING:** It is an ideal place for meditation and listening to our intuition. It can help focus your energies so you can quieten your thoughts and listen to messages from your own inner being or from the spirit realms.
- **GIVING THANKS:** We need a place to celebrate and give thanks to the spirits. Prayers of gratitude are important and allowing yourself to be grateful for the goodness in your life creates a magnetic attraction for even more blessings to come into your life.

My South American neighbour has an altar in her spare room with images of the Madonna as well as family photographs. She told me that when she was very young her grandmother sat at the kitchen table, always in the same chair, which was her place, and gathered together all her sacred objects such as devotional images and her rosary. Her favourite saint was St Anthony and each morning she would pray and sometimes perform small rituals such as placing drops of oil in a saucer of water to assure her family's health. She would also light candles and place gifts of flowers and food on the shrine. If anyone was in trouble she would pray and offer money or gifts to the saint called upon to help solve the problem.

Setting up Your Altar

First you must decide where to put your altar. Many people make their altar in the main lounge area, or have a specific room in the house for spiritual practise. An old fireplace is

often an ideal spot for an altar, but choose wherever feels appropriate to you. Now spend some time thinking about how you want it to look and what overall feeling you wish to portray. Begin to gather the objects to be included and spend time in setting it up. This is a very important step because the basic energy of the foundation of your altar is established through this period.

An altar should have three components: something that represents the divine/God, something that represents your human life and something that represents your connection with the spirit world. All objects on an altar work as catalysts for the inner places within us, so each item that you place on your altar should have meaning and significance for you. Take time to notice your feelings about every object and ensure they are consistent with the intention behind your altar. The choice of objects that can be placed on an altar is virtually limitless – rocks, feathers, wood, bones, shells, metals, crystals, plants and flowers, fruits and grains, herbs, religious icons, ancient deities, essential oils, incense, pictures of family and pets, ancestral items, special gifts, candles, symbolic shapes and patterns – because each object need only be symbolic to your life.

It is now time to decide how you will arrange the objects on the altar. This should be done in a caring and conscientious way. You can either use a logical approach (for instance, placing smaller things in front and larger items at the back or grouping objects according to a theme) or use your intuition. If you are using an intuitive approach, simply place your chosen objects on the altar and then move them about until it feels right. Use whatever method works for you and you will create a meaningful balance.

Bring in the Spirit of Your Altar

Once the altar has been set up, it is time for its dedication ceremony – this brings life into the altar space. This is a kind of initiation rite and can be as simple as lighting a candle and sitting quietly for a few moments and allowing the spirit of your altar to fill your mind and heart. Alternatively, you could ring a bell and let your prayers follow the sound. The dedication ceremony invokes the energy into the altar so that it will radiate out into your home and life. When you have dedicated your space ask your guardian spirits to protect your energy, the spirit of your altar and sacred space. Light a candle and leave a gift on your altar for your spirit guardians. It is important to maintain your altar by regularly meditating and praying there, as the power of your prayers and meditations infuse the altar with energy. Another method of tending the energy is by adding objects, lighting candles and communicating with the space on a daily basis. Keeping the space clean and regularly burning incense helps to enliven the energy of your altar. And, of course, don't forget to make offerings. These express your gratitude for the help and support that you receive from Spirit and demonstrate your open relationship with the spiritual realms.

The Work Altar

To set up the altar at work you just need to carve out a bit of sacred space in the office, no matter how small or unobtrusive. It is an important reminder of the various stresses that we encounter at work, particularly the separation of sacred and profane, the mind and spirit, and the professional and personal, none of which are helpful if we intend to live productive, fulfilled and spiritually rewarding lives. Therefore, it is up to us to create a sacred space at work that can at least unify some of these polarities.

A sense of the sacred can be integrated into your workspace in many different ways. In more formal, corporate settings, a grouping of objects with personal resonance and meaning can provide you with a place of quiet, where, in the course of a hectic working day, you can take a deep inner breath. This is particularly important if you work in an ultramodern building where you are literally cut off from the natural world by air-conditioning and permanently closed windows. Try bringing in something that reminds you of nature's beauty; a single flower in the smallest of vases can serve as a focal point. Create a place for incense and candles for when the space gets too tense and frenetic. Use this space to put your chosen specific crystals to protect your energy from the telephone and computer – crystals dissipate some of the harmful ions coming off these modern but very necessary machines.

The workplace altar does not have to be large to be effective. Begin by looking carefully at the space in which you sit. What do you usually look at? Is the space conducive to productivity or is it dingy and depressing? Try to treat the space as if it matters to you. Pick a spot where you can literally turn away from your work for a moment to rest your eyes and your spirit during the workday. If you work in an office with a window use the windowsill for your altar it has the added benefit of opening vistas in a literal sense. You can choose objects for your altar that remind you of the things within you and in your life that nurture your spirit: a few fresh flowers, natural objects such as a shell, a crystal, a photograph of a guru, an image of Kuan Yin who is the goddess of compassion, or snake for energy and transformation – any object with personal resonance will help.

House Healing

Clearing Negative Energy from Your Home

We are all affected by the energy in our home, so it is important to make it as conducive as possible. A home should be a haven, somewhere that protects you from the world. If you feel your house does not fulfil this purpose then it may be the result of negative energy.

Everything in the universe is made up of energy. Referred to as *chi* by the Chinese, *ki* by the Japanese and *prana* by the peoples of India, this energy permeates our homes affecting the atmosphere and those who live there. Your health, relationships and work can all be affected by the flow of energy through your home or by the build up of negative forces in certain areas.

Space clearing is a method of rebalancing the energy of the home. Some people carry out space clearing once a month but once a year is just as good. However, there are certain circumstances where it is advisable to space clear:

- When you move into a new home
- When you move to a new office or start a new job
- When you and your family are going through a period of bad luck or when everything appears to be going wrong
- When you have finished a relationship and that person is no longer in your life
- After illness
- After a robbery or break-in or any upsetting or disturbing experience in the home

Psychic and Spiritual Spring-clean

At least once a year, cleanse and clean your entire home. The two weeks before the Spring Equinox, which is March 21-23, is an ideal time. It is advisable to wash all windows, inside and out. Take everything out of the drawers and cupboards and clean inside them. Wash all floors and take rugs outside for an airing, or take them to the cleaners – it is a good idea to do the same with bedding and duvets. Dust the top of cupboards, get rid of everything you don't need – pass it on to someone or give it to charity. Anything in your home that you don't love or use any more pulls down the energy of the home. Fix things that need fixing, decorate and bring in something new. This is also the ideal time to clear the garden and plant new plants for the coming summer.

This annual spring clean sets the energy for the year and once a month, preferably around the full moon, you can do a mini cleanse just to refresh the energy of the home.

Can Anybody Clear Energy?

In order to carry out space clearing it is obviously useful to be able to sense the atmosphere or energy in your home to some degree. However, the more you practise, the more you will develop an acute awareness and sensitivity to the energies around you. I have seen excellent clearing conducted by people who believe that they cannot feel or sense energy or atmospheres, so have a bit self-belief. If your intention is focused on clearing the energies of a room then that intention is felt in the room very strongly – even if you cannot consciously feel it. The power of the subconscious mind and your higher self will direct your movements in clearing your space. Gradually, sensing atmospheres will become easier. Just as exercising a muscle makes it stronger, so the mind will become accustomed to the sensation of touching energy.

The Space Clearer's Toolkit

When we space clear we use our ability to sense energy, but in order to clear the energy we need various techniques and tools. Understanding the different tools enables you to decide what you like working with.

SOUND

The power of sound is used to clear and uplift the energy of a room. When atoms are in harmony the sounds produced are pure and melodious but when the atmosphere is chaotic the sounds produced are jarring and strained. Sound can be used to soothe the energies of the atoms in any living space causing them to become balanced and harmonious. I have always used music to clear and uplift energy – from the use of Tibetan bells and singing bowls, to enhancing the power from the earth using a drum with a four beat drum sequence. The sounds either bring to the surface the negative or positive atmosphere of each room, in addition to aggravating any unnatural/dysfunctional negativity which may be below the surface of our day-to-day lifestyle. If you play music into the corners of a room you build the sound until it reaches a frequency that moves the energy.

The following sound tools can be used in space clearing.

- Singing or chanting – for instance the Buddhist mantra OM MANI PADME OM
- Clapping your hands to clear stagnant energy
- Tibetan bells or singing bowls

THE ELEMENTS

The elements can be used in the following ways to clear space and bring in positive energy:

• Air

Use clapping, rattles, drums and music to clear space. To bring in positive energy use wind-chimes and bells.

• Water

To clear space throw drops of water throughout the room or spray the room with a mister of water and aromatherapy oil (see page 126). To bring in positive energy introduce a fountain, waterfall or fish tank.

• Fire

Burn Epsom salts and alcohol to cleanse a very negative atmosphere. Alternatively, burn candles, herbs in a pot, smudge the room or burn incense – either as sticks or in a charcoal burner. To bring in positive energy burn candles for seven nights and burn pure incense.

• Earth

Throw salt upwards and downwards into all spaces within the room, leave for 24 hours, then clear up the salt and bury it in the earth with prayers. To bring in positive energy introduce crystals, stones, fossils and plants.

SCENT

Scent is generally used to uplift the atmosphere after the space has been cleared with sound. Any of the following can be used:

• Herbs

Native American: cedarwood, pine, juniper, sage, sweet grass
Arabian: frankincense, myrrh, rose and jasmine
Greek: bay leaves, verbena, juniper, rosemary

• Essential Oils

Tea tree, eucalyptus, rosemary, cedarwood, pine and lemongrass.

• Incense

My favourite incense is Japanese cedarwood and jasmine, but there are hundreds on the market so try a few out at home before you use them in your space clearing kit.

• Sage Bundles

These are used in smudging, the traditional Native American method of using smoke to purify a space (see box, page 149). The most common herbs used are sage, sweetgrass or cedar. Smudge sticks are also available.

Smudging a Room

Smudging is the traditional Native American method of using smoke to purify a space. Smudging is an intuitive art, so let your inner feelings show you what to do and how you should do it.

- To create a smudge smoke, first light the bundle of herbs. When the herbs are ignited, blow the fire out and the bundle will continue to smoke. With your free hand, hold a fireproof bowl underneath the smoking herbs to catch any sparks. First smudge yourself with the smoke from your head down the body to the ground by cuping some smoke into your hand and moving it over your body.

- Now begin to work the smoke from the smouldering stick around the four corners of the room, invoking the powers of the four directions, the earth and the sky and Creator God. Work clockwise starting at the most easterly corner, move the smoke around the walls, make your movements gentle and lift the smoke from the floor to the ceiling before moving into the next corner. If you sense any heavy or sticky areas in the room, take the smoke back into the space and repeat the movement from the floor to the ceiling and gradually the smoke will break up the stagnant energy.

- When you have completed smudging the circumference of the room, stand in the centre and ask Spirit to purify and cleanse the room, say a prayer or chant a mantra as the smoke permeates the atmosphere.

- When you have completed your smudge ceremony, tap the smoking herbs firmly in the bowl until the smoke has died out. (The herbs can continue smouldering for a long time after they have been extinguished so it is very important never to leave them unattended.)

Exploring Each Room Using Your Inner Senses

Before you begin to clear the energy of your home it is essential that you tune in through simple visualization techniques. Begin as you would for any of the visualization techniques and then journey through one room at a time with your imagination/vision. Sense what you feel about each area and write down your impressions. You can do this technique before each space clearing ritual that you conduct.

Check out the following areas:

1 Clutter
2 Objects
3 Cupboards
4 Electrical equipment
5 Hallways
6 Walls

Note: Always remember to do your 'inner preparation' before exploring and always remember to 'close' when you have finished working.

Ground Rules on Space Clearing

- Focus on what you are doing and why you are clearing your space.

- It is recommended that you begin your work from your sacred space room (see chapter on sacred space) to link in with the powers within your home and to connect you with your inner self and the protection from your guardian spirits and ancestors.

- Be very relaxed and understand that this practice will not release any spirits, you are clearing the energies around you and not praying or invoking or releasing any spirit forms.

- Undertake all space clearing activities in the morning after the sun has come out, as this is the most energetic time of day for bringing light and power into the ritual. It is recommended that you do not conduct space clearing after the sun sets or on overcast or rainy days as the dullness within the day will not encourage a positive energy clearing session.

- Do not perform space clearing rituals for other people until you are very experienced or qualified in the art of space clearing. You will find the energy from other people's property will be disturbed by your actions, which in turn may affect your own energy. It is best that you recommend how to do a ritual and then let them get on with it themselves.

- In space clearing you are addressing only the energy of a place not the spirits that live there, so make sure that you focus your intent. Complete the ritual by ending where you began and then close off your focus and let the ritual take care of releasing the energy.

- Before you begin, ensure that no one else will be around and that you will be able to work without interruption. Check the house has had a general spring clean – there is no point cleansing the energy if the room or space is untidy, filled with clutter, debris and rubbish.

- Before clearing any space always bring yourself into a calm state of mind. Go into your sacred room and sit quietly. Let yourself relax, ground and guide yourself into a relaxation meditation. Then, when you are feeling calm, allow yourself to get a sense of the space and the organization of the clearing ritual.

Space Clearing Exercise

- Choose one room at a time. Go to the centre of the room and call upon the power of protection and cleansing. Be aware that each room will have a different atmosphere so you must conduct a full ritual in each room before moving on into the next one.

- Begin to follow the energy around your room by moving into each corner using your bells or Tibetan bowl. Ring the bells until you feel that the sound has had an effect on the atmosphere. You need to trust that it has had an effect, even if you are not sensitive. Work with the power of sound and move the energy upwards and out of the corners, following the room around until complete.

- Next take a bowl of sea salt, throw the salt upwards and back down into each corner of the room (leave the salt for 24 hours before clearing it up and then bury it outside in the earth).

- Next burn sage or incense. Take it into each corner and bring the smoke upwards towards the ceiling then move gently around the room until you have covered the four corners.

- Finally use holy or purified water with added essential oils, preferably tea tree which is very cleansing. Sprinkle the water into the four corners then upwards towards the ceiling. Then move around the room back to where you began. Place the bowl of water in the centre of the room for 24 hours before pouring the water outside into the earth.

- Complete your cleansing programme by placing natural quartz crystals that have been programmed for cleansing (refer to the crystals section) into each corner. Leave them there for 24 hours and then wash and cleanse the crystals and replace them with crystals which have been programmed for protection. Leave them in the four corners for a month before you wash and cleanse them. This seals the protective energy that has been brought into your space.

The Workplace

As you will by now recognize, we are all much more influenced by atmospheres than we realize. It is vital, therefore, that in addition to our home environment we must give careful consideration to the space where we work. After all, we spend up to 60 hours a week at work, so it has a considerable influence on our mental, physical, emotional and spiritual well-being.

A bad atmosphere can be caused by the environmental pollution inherent in a 'sick building', but it can also be the result of the building becoming 'haunted' due to its malevolent history. The energy becomes excessively negative, especially when there has been illness or death, or

if the building has been a prison, hospital, war-torn zone or a place of violence or drugs. All these activities can cause an atmosphere to become blocked. Such buildings must be cleared before a healthy and balanced space can be restored. Space clearing, however, is not only appropriate for badly afflicted buildings – it is a means of making space as conducive as possible to our energies and what we wish to achieve. For this reason it is advisable to conduct a space clearing ritual as soon as you begin a new job at a new location and annually.

Davina Mackail has provided the following guidance on space clearing within the workplace.

Space Clearing Your Workplace

The following technique can be used for both home and office space. A word of warning before we begin: do not underestimate the power of this work; it needs to be undertaken with respect. I have spent many years working with a variety of traditions, teachers and clients using different space clearing rituals and the following is a condensed ritual for cleansing space. It is a powerful and transformational tool that you can use effectively within the guidelines expressed here. This technique can be used safely by the inexperienced clearer on their personal home office space. If you run a small business with less than five employees it is also safe. Likewise you can use it if you have your own private office within a larger corporation – providing of course you get permission as the use of incense and candles are a potential fire risk and a magnet for smoke alarms.

I would not recommend you use this technique to clear other people's space, as you do not necessarily wish to open yourself up to their 'issues'. Similarly if you are in charge of a large organization I would recommend you call in a professional space clearer, as they will be more psychically able to handle the different energies and issues from all the people working there. They will also be detached from any personal issues and so be able to clear the space with the intent of making it work for the highest good of all concerned.

Timing

Set a date for your space clearing ceremony. Certain times are better than others: between a new moon and full moon is helpful for clearing a space ready for new business or clients, while the time between a full moon and the next new moon is best for ridding a space of particularly negative energy or bad 'predecessor chi' – for example, if the previous occupant's business failed in some way. Do not space clear at night as the energy is at its lowest ebb – mornings are definitely best. If you are female I would not recommend space clearing during menstruation. Similarly it is not recommended that you clear a space if you are feeling ill, recovering from illness or are feeling physically debilitated or under par energy-wise.

Focus Your Intent

Before you start, it is important to understand the energetic process that you are about to begin. Clearing a space creates a hole or vacuum. If you do not fill that space with your new wishes, you will simply get back what you've tried to clear out. So the first step is to be very clear about why you are space clearing. What is your intention? If you are clearing out an office because you've had a lot of bad debt then your intention will be to ensure the space is filled with abundance and people paying their bills on time. This intent is the most important aspect of the entire ceremony. The rest is about providing the most powerful and focused channel for this intention to become manifest.

So once you have set the date take time to focus on your intent. Sit in your sacred space, ground your energy and connect to your higher wisdom as you contemplate first what you wish to clear from the space and then what you choose to bring into that space. Write a list and ensure that the intentions are positive. Language is a powerful tool in the process of manifestation so ensure that you use your words carefully. For example, if you make the statement 'I want more money' that is exactly what you will get – the experience of 'wanting' more money, rather than the money itself. We are our own creators so activate that creative force by stating 'I choose to have more money' instead.

Clean Up Your Workplace

A few days before the ceremony the office needs to be physically cleared of all clutter and cleaned thoroughly. Although this task may seem like a laborious and unnecessary chore, if you approach it with a joyful attitude and with your intent in mind it can be surprisingly uplifting and inspiring as you start to feel the shift in energy from these early stages of the process. If you space clear without physically cleaning your space first you can cause unnecessary chaos in your life, as the cleansing process will magnify what is there, i.e. clutter.

Prepare Yourself

In my experience when you engage in the process of clearing with a powerful intent the purging effect can also happen on a corresponding level in your physical self. So, on occasion it is possible to suffer a bout of diarrhoea or flu-like symptoms after a particularly powerful

clearing. This is nature's way of clearing out our internal junk and providing symptoms do not become excessive or persistent is perfectly safe and extremely cleansing. To minimize these possible side effects drink at least 2-3 litres of water the day before, during and after the clearing and take an Epsom salt bath after the clearing ritual has been completed. You may also feel excessively tired following the ritual – again this is just your body adjusting to the energetic shift so harmonize with this and book an early night rather than a wild party.

The Ritual

Gather all the necessary tools before you begin. You will need natural rock salt, a shell, a large feather, a smaller feather, candles, flowers, crystals or rocks of your choice, an altar cloth, a drum, a rattle, a bell or Tibetan bells or bowl, cedarwood incense or a white sage bundle, a charcoal and incense burner, matches, plant spray filled with holy water and flower essences or a few drops of lavender oil, bay leaves, food and spirit offerings for the ancestors and 'hungry ghosts'.

1 Remove all jewellery and watches as metal items can absorb the negative energies you are trying to clear, and put away all food and drink that may be lying around for the same reason. Turn off your telephone and make sure you will be undisturbed. If you have animals they often like to be involved and may follow you around while you work. I would recommend, however, that you leave babies and small children with a carer while you carry out this work.

2 Set up your altar on a table in the power spot of the space. This can be the centre of the main room or any space that you feel is 'right' to work from. Lay out the altar cloth and use a compass to find the four cardinal directions. In the south place a rock or crystal to focus your grounding. This should be where you stand to work from (i.e. you have the rock nearest to you on the table). In the north, place a feather to represent the spirit world. In the east place a candle to represent the world of the intellect and the mind, and in the west place a shell or glass of water to represent the emotional world. In the centre of these four directions place your written intentions as a reminder of your intent throughout the process. Put food and flower offerings in the north to appease the ancestors and spirit world, you can also pour them a glass of alcohol. (After the ritual place the offerings under a tree in the garden or a place of nature. Do not eat them.) Place all the other objects you will use on the altar cloth around the circumference of the central directions. If I am clearing a house or an office space with many rooms I may make individual offerings for each of the rooms consisting of some flower petals sprinkled with holy water, an incense stick and a candle. But this is entirely optional.

3 First light a candle, then spend some time getting into a relaxed meditative state (see section 2, pages 23–29).

4 Spend a few minutes grounding your energy and doing some deep breathing techniques. If you have a particular breathing technique you use then that is fine – I use the following empowering breath to focus my energy for the task ahead.

5 Kneel on the floor sitting on your heels. Raise your head to the sky and breathe in through the nose, lower your head to the floor and breathe out through the mouth. Repeat three times. On the fourth breath hold the inhalation and push the air down into your hara, take three small 'top-up' breaths to ensure your lungs are at maximum capacity then relax while still holding the breath. When you feel ready, release the breath slowly. Do three rounds of this. Now take a final deep inhale, hold, focus your intent on empowering your heart chakra and then exhale while imagining the power of that breath energizing your inner being.

6 Connect to your guides and spirit helpers and ask for them to assist you in the ceremony you are about to perform. Also ask for the blessing of the office diva for the greatest good of all to be brought into your space. If you are not used to working with guides ask the four major Archangels to help you: Archangel Michael the protector of the north, Raphael the protector of the west, Uriel the protector of the east and Gabriel the guardian of the south. Angels love to be asked and will always come to your assistance.

7 Take the natural rock salt and sprinkle a line at each entrance to the space – this forms a protective ring of purification around the office. The salt will help absorb the negative energies that you clear out and should be left *in situ* overnight before sweeping up and disposing of. Open a window or two to help the negative vibrations escape.

8 Using the drum, start from the front door and walk around the entire inner circumference of the space in a clockwise direction, drumming loudly. Make sure you work into all the corners of the space and under desks and chairs. The beat of the drum is perfect for clearing through the denser layers of energy that have become stagnant in your space. If you don't have a drum, loud clapping or even shouting will do. Finish the circuit at your altar in the south position.

9 Feathers are fantastic for sensing pockets of stagnant or negative energy. Use a large feather which has been smudged beforehand with cedarwood (the feather should be used only for this purpose). Walk round the space 'stroking' the feather from the top to the bottom of the walls in a large, slow, sweeping motion. You are not actually touching the wall but are very close to it. When you feel the feather get stuck or sense that it is hard to push through a certain area that seems dense, stop and spend a few moments sweeping with the feather to clear the stagnant energy (if you have an altar, sweep towards the direction of your altar).

10 Next, take the incense burner and burn some cedarwood or a bundle of white sage and walk round the space again. You can use the feather to gently waft the smoke into all the corners and dark spaces of the rooms. Both cedarwood and white sage are used by shamanic traditions as powerful purification herbs and are the final check in ensuring the space has been thoroughly cleansed of its negative and stagnant vibrations.

11 Now wash your hands, close the windows and seal the space. Stand in the middle of the room (or at your altar) and imagine a large bubble of white or golden energy completely encasing the space. This bubble should go over the roof and under the ground. For extra protection you can imagine the outer surface of the bubble as having a shiny metal surface to deflect any negativity. You are now ready to start filling the space with your positive intentions.

12 Read through your intentions once more then gather up three bay leaves. The bay leaf is from the same plant family as the sacred cocoa leaf used in South American shamanic traditions. It is used to carry your prayers to Spirit and fill your space with your positive vibrations. The three leaves represent the three worlds: the upper world of spirit, the lower world of the earth and the middle world of the human that connects the other two. Hold the three leaves together between the thumb and the first finger of your right hand and blow your intentions into the leaves. When you feel strongly connected to your positive intentions for the space do another circuit of the space blowing your prayers through the leaves into the space as you go. Always use fresh bay leaves for each clearing. The old ones should be dispensed with by burying them in the garden as an offering to mother earth or burning them as an offering to father heaven. You dispose of them in this way to energetically let go of your attachment to the outcome of the clearing. You have offered up your prayers of intention to the universe and should then detach and leave it to the source to bring you your answers in whatever way is for the greatest good of all concerned.

13 Lastly, take the plant spray filled with holy water and flower essences or lavender oil and walk around the space spraying into the corners and centre of the room. This 'sets' your intentions and helps take them deep into the fabric of the space.

14 Now the ritual has finished thank your guides, spirit helpers, the office diva, the Archangels and anybody else you asked to assist you in your work. It is also advisable to allow the candle to burn out. You may like to play your favourite music once a space clearing has been completed to enhance the positive vibrations.

Please be aware that just occasionally things need to get worse before they get better. Although the majority of people experience an immediate and positive reaction to a clearing, sometimes a clearing can cause a rush of seemingly 'bad' events that will perhaps make you doubt the process. All this means is that the process has raised to the surface issues that need a final clearing before the good vibrations can take effect. Relax and do not become attached to these negative events; they will soon pass and with hindsight you will understand why things needed to be that way.

Welcoming Nature into the Home

As you begin to change your home to become more of a reflection of your soul you will probably find, like many other people, that nature starts to creep in. Modern buildings and homes are often separated from nature and the sensation of being in such a place also makes us feel disconnected. However, as we uncover our psychic and spiritual side we begin to realize our inherent connection with nature and how much poorer we are for neglecting that relationship.

To begin to correct that balance we can not only go out and seek a connection with nature but we can bring it into our homes. One of the simplest ways to do this is to welcome natural objects into your home. Natural objects recall ancestral memories of early times when we lived close to the land. In our conservatory we have rocks, feathers – including the children's treasured objects such as abandoned birds nests – funny shaped logs from the local forest and unusual shaped stones plus crystals, rocks … These objects are not just intrinsically beautiful, they are a constant reminder of our place on the planet and how important it is to be grounded in the earth.

If you have a garden, this provides a wonderful opportunity to have a deep relationship with nature – a beautiful place where we feel peace and connection. The garden is often the first place where many of us learn about nature and the power it has to help us with our spirituality, our healing and our self-awareness. But, like any spiritual work, it can't just be done once and then forgotten; it is a daily process that makes the magic happen in your garden.

Building a Shrine in the Garden

There are many ways of creating sacred space outside and of celebrating and honouring the sacred in nature. Many people regard their gardens as part of their sacred space, a place where they are put in touch with the energy of growth and where they participate in the miracle of nature. Even the simple act of digging the earth seems to connect us to the ancient rhythms of nature: the scent, texture and colour of the soil combine to wake us up and centre us. The forms of life we discover hidden amid the earth, the earthworms, beetles and bugs are a small epiphany of the unseen web of nature. The miracle of life is celebrated in planting the seed and watching it bloom. Even a garden that is dying off during the winter teaches us to focus and slow down; growth has its own timetable. Gardening makes us mindful of the elements and the power of the sun, and puts us back in touch with the mother earth.

Building altars or shrines outside permits us to celebrate and honour our connection with nature. It is an act of expression that brings thoughts and feelings from a deeper soul reality into a physical reality and permits us to truly see who we are.

Begin by really looking at your surroundings. What does the natural landscape say to you? What is its spirit? Use your intuition and you will naturally be drawn to a particular part of your garden. When setting up a shrine you have to decide, as with your home altar, the three main objectives: what will represent the divine, what will represent nature and what will represent humanity. Beautiful objects from nature – stones, crystals, driftwood, fossils, shells, etc – are all natural choices but you can also include things that have not been shaped by

nature. Anything made by hand, by an artist or crafts person, has a soul. The object will contain the spirit of the artist who created it and sometimes the spirit of the natural material it was made from.

It is also useful to represent the four elements and place them in the four directions appropriate to their power positions in astrological calendars, i.e. earth in the north, air in the east, fire in the south and water in the west. You could also have symbols representing the four seasons and use the symbol of the season as it arises throughout the year with seasonal plants or symbols representing this time. This reminds you to keep connected with the earth and the rhythms of nature.

Many people dedicate their shrine to an icon. An icon is a sacred relic; usually a painting, weaving or bejewelled carving that depicts an image of a holy figure in a symbolic, highly stylized manner. The artist or crafts person can follow a precise design format and with personal, spiritual intention creates a piece of art that becomes sacred. These precious icons become imbued with meaning and sometimes are even associated with miracles through prayer. An icon is a 'doorway to heaven' for sacred communication. Gardens can become our own personalized icon, if we can create them with intention and imbue them with our love and personal meaning, these small patches of land will in turn radiate their own spirit.

Some places on the Earth are touched with the Great Spirit, a powerful spiritual energy that emanates from a place. These particular spots have been called sacred for thousands of years by indigenous peoples. However, a sacred connection can occur in almost any natural environment; we can re-sanctify the land around our home by introducing our own spiritual connection and awakening our connection to the sacred. Any garden has this potential – and the ability to restore and cultivate a personalized view of how creation can represent paradise.

Energetic and psychic Disturbances

The vibrations you are exposed to in your surroundings affect your health and interfere with your system energetically. You therefore have to take care of your energy as much as you take care of your body. Although it is not always possible you should always try to choose environments that lift your energy, rather than drain or lower your vibrations. You cannot always do this but being aware of your own sensitivity is essential in psychic awareness.

Detection and Diagnosis of Energy and Atmosphere

There are various problems that could be the cause of negative energy in your environment.

Geopathic Stress

Geopathic stress is a form of electromagnetic pollution caused by such things as underground streams, geological faults, railway cuttings, etc. The earth has its own electromagnetic field, which resonates at a frequency of approximately 7.83 Hz – the same frequency as human brain waves. When this field becomes distorted it can affect those living in its path. Geopathic stress is particularly harmful when it crosses an area where we spend a considerable amount of time, for instance the bedroom or living room.

As geopathic stress travels in lines it tends to affect certain areas of the home, consequently it may only affect one member of the household if they habitually work or sleep in the affected area. Some of the signs of geopathic stress include illness, irritability and long-term tiredness. Geopathic stress can be detected by dowsing (you can try this yourself or contact a professional). Details on the history of the site of your home – for instance are there any underground streams, is it on the site of an old quarry – can also uncover clues. Also, look to your children and pets: dogs, babies and young children instinctively shy away from areas with geopathic stress while cats love it!

Space clearing consultant Susie Zgorska related the following story from one of her clients.

A young couple bought a house together but within three weeks moved out due to the woman becoming incredibly ill, being generally uneasy, feeling very cold and crying all the time. They contacted Susie in desperation. Tuning into the house she uncovered two lingering spirits and a good deal of geopathic stress. It was also discovered that the previous occupants had only stayed a year before moving out due to money troubles and ill health. Susie helped the spirits move on and used crystals to rebalance the earth energies. She then space cleared to remove any last vestiges of negative predecessor chi and cultivate a sacred environment that would support and nurture the young couple.

A month later Susie received a letter from the couple expressing their profound thanks for putting their world back to rights. The crying and ill health had stopped and they finally felt peaceful and happy in their new home.

A method similar to acupuncture is used to cure geopathic stress. Just as the body has meridians of energy that can be blocked, causing energy to stagnate, so the earth has a similar grid of energy veins that can become stagnant. 'Earth acupuncture' – which can be done using natural wood wands, copper stakes or natural crystals – is the answer, but it does require the skills of an expert (see Resources, page 180).

Positive Ions

As well as being affected by large-scale energy faults, we are also at the mercy of the gadgetry of the modern home and office. Most electrical equipment – computers, clocks, radios, photocopiers, microwaves and mobile phones – release positive ions into the air. These can make us irritable, aggressive, unwell, cause headaches, migraines, allergies and digestive and respiratory disorders.

How to disperse positive ions:

- Walk barefoot on the grass
- Cleanse your aura or your room by spraying water mixed with 3–4 drops of pine or cypress essential oil. You can add some sea salt to this mixture for an extra cleansing effect
- Buy an ioniser for work and home
- Some people choose to have miniature pump action waterfalls in their homes

Negative ions, in contrast, make us feel good and are a great antidote to the positive ions we are constantly bombarded with. Negative ions are plentiful around running water – for instance waterfalls and streams – and mountains.

Sick Building Syndrome

This problem commonly occurs when a house is built on reclaimed land, marsh, fen or mud flats. The goodness and well-being of the property is effectively drawn through the foundations in to the earth. This affects not only the house but the people who live there – sapping vital energy and, in some cases, causing stress, fatigue and a general apathy. This type of problem can cause both body and spirit to feel affected by the sickness in the building. These conditions may also exist when a house is built on an old graveyard or burial ground, inviting the additional problems of living in a haunted house.

If, having investigated and tackled these possible causes of negative energy you still have a problem with one room or part of the house, then it's time to ask if your home may be haunted.

Ghosts and Earthbound Spirits

It is always advisable before you move house to check out your proposed home in the local archives to discover what the site was used for in the past. The most negative places are often old hospitals, mental asylums, plague pits, burial sites, even pubs or hotels that were frequented by the local population.

The memories of the past have a habit of overlapping with the present, affecting the property's current use. In some cases there is a residential ghost or earthbound spirit which for one reason or another coexists with the living residents – and they are often very capable of contact and interfering with the lives of anyone living in the property.

EARTHBOUND SPIRITS

Many souls seek to live as they did when they were alive, despite the spirit world gently coercing them into letting go of their identity from this life. It is these types of personalities that become possessed with a desire to remain in the physical world and get their own way – whatever the cost.

It takes a house doctor, soul rescuer or exorcist with experience in hauntings to eliminate a malevolent force or a tricky earthbound spirit, but with simpler hauntings it is often possible to clear the spirit out without having to call in a specialist.

Therese, an artist and close friend, had a house entity that would move through from the property next door into her living room during the evening. You could feel when he had come into the house as the atmosphere in the evening was heavy, while during the day it was much lighter. He would move around the property and on some occasions would aggravate her two-year-old daughter when she was asleep. He would draw from her energy and when he did this she would immediately wake up screaming out 'leave me alone'.

One night we decided to communicate with him as he was becoming a serious nuisance. There were three of us having supper, including a girlfriend Taryn. I called the entity to come and join us and I felt him being drawn in to our auras. I asked Taryn to permit herself to be the host to his energy. She trusted me enough to place herself in this unusual and dangerous position. I then asked Therese to hold Taryn's hands to help bring him in. This was to make sure that he remained magnetically attached so he wouldn't disappear before we had a chance to rescue him. He was very clever and knew all the ghostly tricks of moving through space on the astral level and I knew he would try and escape.

When I could see him in Taryn I began to communicate with him about his life and why he was still here. It transpired that he was lonely and that he meant no harm, that he loved Therese's little girl but she was frightened of him. He missed his family so we called upon his ancestors to come and help him find them. The moment the spirits arrived the lights in the room appeared to be much brighter as if we had lit several large church candles in the centre of the room. He was lifted out of Taryn's aura. I closed Taryn down and we said prayers of protection and then lit candles and smudged the room with sage. We never felt his presence again and Therese's daughter began to sleep through the night with no more screaming night terrors.

WARNING Never attempt to channel or allow a spirit or being in any way to take over your aura or your physical body unless you are fully experienced or are in the hands of a competent, well-trained and sensible teacher.

GHOSTS

There are tales of ghosts, spooks and hauntings the world over. While some are fictional, others appear to be true. In general a ghost is thought to be someone who lived on earth, but when the body died the spirit remained or was bound to the earth.

Paranormal research suggests that in many cases they are not souls of the dead but rather telepathic messages from their lingering bodiless minds or, in simple terms, memories. Another theory is that ghosts are not dead people's souls but are instead projections from objects and buildings that have absorbed psychic energy and these psychic impressions are then broadcast back to people who enter the vicinity or use the object with the psychic energy of the previous owner. The clarity of these images is said to depend on the emotional force of the original psychic imprint, as well as the psychic sensitivity of the recipient. This leads to the conclusion that this is why certain people feel energy and a psychic presence in a place while others are insensitive to it.

Some researchers suggest that these psychic impressions play back over and over again like a psychic tape, believing that the ghost is a psychic projection of a sensitive person's mind when they are responding to the telepathic residue left in the atmosphere.

Although all of the theories about ghosts sound possible, and may explain some of the psychic phenomena that we experience, I am inclined to take the traditional view that a ghost in the majority of cases is someone's soul that has become earthbound for any number of reasons.

Ghosts appear and reappear again and again and are seen by numerous people. Typical examples are the wispy mists seen only out of the corner of your eye, or as various solid-looking figures which mysteriously disappear in front of you. They tend not to follow people from house to house, as they are usually associated with a particular location rather than a particular person.

It should be noted that the world of ghosts or spirits does not coexist within our own linear time zone. Whereas we know the time of day, week, year, etc., quite often the spirit wanders around caught up in a time warp. Thus ghosts are often sighted in period costume. Although this is not always the case it is common in many old properties.

The most traditional belief about ghosts is that when they died they were either too attached to the earth and therefore didn't want to leave their property, family or partner; or

that they died a sudden death and are in a state of confusion, not having realized that they are dead. These types of ghosts are generally ancestors – family spirits who wish to be involved in the protection and guidance of their descendents. In some cases these souls are very helpful and supportive; in other cases, when the spirits have not evolved spiritually, they tend to dominate, forcing their opinion and points of view on family members. They can cause serious conflicting atmospheres and arguments among family members, creating mental and physical problems aggravated by their presence.

HELPFUL GHOSTS

This is usually a spirit who once lived and experienced all of life's ups and downs, had a family and lived a happy life, so when they passed into the spirit world they decided to guide and support the living – either family, friends or students.

UNHELPFUL GHOSTS

Many people have had a psychic experience or know someone who has had one with a ghost. More often than not they are encountering unhelpful ghosts, the troubled and aggressive type of ghost who is still caught up with whatever tragedy affected their life. This is often the more sinister malevolent type of ghost who lurks in graveyards, haunted castles, stately homes, hotels and ancient relics. They are the ghosts that are very aware of the living and can cause psychic manifestations that can terrify the person witnessing their antics.

POLTERGEISTS

The poltergeist is a complicated source of psychic energy that can demonstrate and disrupt by causing physical phenomena. It has the strength to move objects and furniture around, including lifting human beings and throwing them across the room. People have felt a ghost attack them in their sleep, usually the sensation is one of being paralyzed and feeling that they are awake but unable to move their body because of a weighty sensation across their chests. This is a typical symptom of poltergeist activity.

APPARITIONS

The opposite side of the coin to the poltergeist is an apparition. This is a spectre or phantom, known to have no consciousness. These are ghosts usually noted for appearing then just as quickly disappearing, passing through walls or dissolving in front of your eyes. These quirks of nature are usually an imprint on the ether, which may represent a past event, phantom figures which in their time could have been regarded as a larger-than-life character.

The apparition is an imprint on the earth's memory which, for one reason or another, is released into the physical atmosphere to be witnessed by people today – in the same way that we may recall our own experiences many years later to share with our family and friends.

Recognizing a Ghost

Usually the best way to tell if your home has a ghost, even if you don't actually see it, is to trust your feelings. If there is an area of your home that always feels cool or damp, and there is no physical source of the coldness, this could be evidence of the presence of a ghost. If there is a location in your home where you feel physically heavy and where it is more difficult to breathe or you feel a heaviness on your neck and shoulders, this can also indicate an earthbound spirit.

In our home we have a spirit of an old lady who sits in what was her downstairs parlour. She has disturbed people who have stayed with us and on a couple of occasions our cleaners have commented on the atmosphere of this particular room. However, there is nothing to fear from ghosts, they cannot hurt you – particularly if you are not afraid of them. Nevertheless, I believe it is better to have a house with no unwanted guests and the happiest ghosts are those who have been given the opportunity to move into the higher spiritual realms.

Ghost Busting

In my apprenticeship years, I trained with various psychics but my greatest teacher was my husband Terry. I spent many years travelling with him, visiting sacred sites, ancient places and people's properties in order to tune in to their atmospheres and learn how to detect and release ghosts.

This is Terry's advice on how to deal with a haunting.

'For a successful clearing you need a level of sensitivity which will enable you to 'tune in'. A ghost can be detected in many ways: the trained expert may see a ghost as a physical presence while others may hear voices which appear from an invisible source. Others hear unusual noises – creaky floorboards and breathing noises – when no one is around. Not everyone will witness a ghost, even if they are sensitive to the atmosphere of a haunting.

A ghost (disembodied spirit) tends to make a beeline for a sensitive person, attempting to absorb the magnetic energy of the body as well as the warmth of their body heat. This is why people who have encounters with psychic phenomena feel a coldness or a chill across their skin like a cold wind. A ghost may move from place to place, hiding like a naughty child. While some spirits invite contact, many avoid it. These can prove to the most difficult to remove, especially if they don't want to leave the property.

Once a ghost is located, the best approach is to sit still and try to make contact with the presence. You don't have to be afraid of communicating with a ghost but only conduct this exercise if you have confidence in your own psychic ability and the protection that you have from the spirit world. Faith in a higher power is essential otherwise fear could result in a situation getting out of control, then you will feel vulnerable to the presence, and this places you in a very weak position.

The best way to help the spirit is with other like-minded friends. Form a circle in the place which is haunted. This is helpful in building some power and establishing a platform from which the spirit may be sent on to the higher spiritual realms. Now establish communication. The best way to do this is simply by speaking out loud your intention. Tell the spirit how it is affecting the household. At this stage you may have to give them proof that they are dead as often they are not aware of this. (Show them a current newspaper or a calendar with the date on it.)

Ask the spirit simple questions such as: when did you last see your wife/husband/family? When did you last leave the house? Where did you go when you did? Don't be afraid of talking to them – they can hear what you are saying. With some they may believe that you are threatening them, ignore this and just continue your communication – they will eventually listen to what you have to say as it is in their best interest.

It is important to establish in the mind of the soul that they have passed over. Many of these souls would have died some years ago and may exhibit a state of shock when shown a current newspaper or calendar with date – even modern music can cause an abrupt realization. Ask them to look into a mirror, breathe on it, touch it with their hands and they will discover that there is no reflection and no marks.

The idea is to establish in the mind of the soul that they have passed over into the spirit world, only then is it possible to help them. The rescue of the spirit is achieved by prayer, asking for help from protective spirits and ancestors, even if you are not sure that your call for assistance is being heard. Many of our students who were unsure of their abilities found

that as soon as they asked with a true purpose then the powers within the spirit world came to assist the rescue. You can then pray for the soul's onward journey.

Visualize the room filled with light, invite either a guardian angel or ancestor to come and escort the spirit away to a place of safety/heaven/paradise (whatever term you feel suitable for the circumstances). When the spirit has left, the cold atmosphere will disappear and a peaceful balance will be restored. (If everything fails and the spirit appears to still be in the property then call the experts.)

After the presence has gone you must conduct a clearing ritual appropriate to spirit release:

1   Open all windows to let out any stale energy
2   Smudge the atmosphere, burning a sage bundle in all the affected rooms
3   Lay unrefined sea salt in the four corners of the affected rooms
4   Use a bell or drum to bring in new energy. Play the instrument around the room, beginning at the four corners
5   Burn essential oils on a burner to clean out the atmosphere and purify the energy
6   Clean and tidy the room, washing curtains or sofa covers, rugs, etc., that may still hold the atmosphere

If the presence doesn't leave it could be connected to something which is in the room or house, something that it has attached to or that belonged to them when they were alive. Examples of items that a spirit presence may be connected to include antiques such as paintings and mirrors; porous items such as clay, leather, silk, velvet material; jewellery; beds; handmade items, and any items that have been used in ritual, sacred or religious acts.

WARNING Be careful in buildings which were formerly used as workhouses, mental asylums, prisons, hospitals, abattoirs, etc. They may be haunted not by spirits but by the atmosphere of suffering and pain. Also be careful where you stay when on holiday or taking a weekend break as many hotels, guest houses and pubs have a long history of being haunted and you are also picking up on the atmosphere of all the other people who have slept in that room.'

Possession and Psychic Attachment

Psychic attachment tends to happen to people whose aura or soul has been affected by trauma. If this trauma is not dealt with (see page 000 on soul loss) it can leave a gap into

which energy can plug or become attached. Spirits lock on to the aura and are drawn into the Etheric web, depending on the size of the opening within the aura.

Many attachments can carry over from childhood when an overprotective parent does not allow the child to develop autonomy, therefore part of the parent may remain attached to the child. In other cases it is due to the influence of an ancestral spirit.

Symptoms of psychic attachment include:

- No vitality
- Feeling your energy is being drained and depleted
- Loss of creativity
- Feeling as though you are living out someone else's life plan or belief
- Making choices that you do not feel are your own
- Feeling as though another energy is attached to you
- Feeling as though someone is looking over your shoulder
- Hearing voices in your head that you know are not yours
- A change in personality
- Feelings of helplessness and powerlessness
- Tightness in the solar plexus
- Unusual anger or irritability
- Unusual desire to eat or drink something which you wouldn't normally eat or drink

Sometimes spirits who attach are actually trying to protect their host from further damage. This is common when people have had a traumatic childhood or lived in a haunted property during their formative years.

Sarah, a wife and mother of two young girls, came to see me for a healing session. When we began working I soon became aware of two spirit entities attached to her lower spine. She had had a weakness in her lower back for many years that caused aching in her knees and hips. She had been tested for arthritis but the results were negative.

I asked her if she remembered an incident in her early childhood where she became frightened and aware of spirits. She recalled that the family had lived in an old house which she felt was haunted. Her family always denied that any psychic phenomena had occurred. I went on to release two spirit entities from her back. They were two old gentlemen, who told me that they wanted to protect her, as she was very sad when she was little. Once they had agreed to move on, with the help of my spirit guardians, the relief on Sarah's face was amazing. She looked five years younger and her back pain disappeared.

She rang me a few days later to let me know that she still felt very well and had asked her mother about her childhood home. There were two brothers who had owned the house before the family moved in, one had died and the other had to go into a nursing home.

While some attachments are personal, others are arbitrary. You may be open and vulnerable at the time they occurred, for example if you were very ill, weak, or traumatized, or upset, drunk, taking drugs, or someone close to you had died ... whatever could cause you not to be fully present in your body. This leaves a gap for the attachment to take place. A damaged aura – whatever the reason – leaves you with an insufficient defence mechanism.

In many cases a sensitive person doesn't always pick up earthbound spirits within their aura, all that happens is that their aura brushes against the spirit and when they move away from the situation they no longer feel the energy from it. Many people never experience a spirit attachment and the people who do tend to be sensitive and have natural psychic powers. This is the reason why spirit entities are drawn into your energy field. The best advice I can offer if this ever happens to you is first do not be afraid as they cannot cause serious harm. Secondly, talk to them and gradually begin to communicate. Finally, practise the exercise on page 166 for clearing an earthbound spirit. The technique works the same whether it is in you or outside of you.

When you feel that the spirit has been released from your aura, light a candle for the soul and clear your energy by using incense or a smudge stick, brushing the smoke against your body until you have smudged your energy field. Complete the release by closing your energy down using the chakra closing technique and then close off your aura by using the cloak method (see page 97).

If you find that you are successful at releasing earthbound entities from your home and yourself, then soul rescuing may be one of your natural psychic gifts.

Working with your gifts

When Spirit calls us to work with our gifts, it totally changes our lives. In past eras, many people sought the help of gifted psychics but few have wished to become one.

When the call to work with psychic powers arises, it is often severely resisted. Eventually, the candidate submits since resistance becomes too difficult to maintain and in some cases can become life threatening. This seemingly coercive spiritual call should be regarded in the same light as that of an artist who says, 'I must create or die!' If we ignore our gifts, we immediately become imbalanced and lose touch with reality, in some cases fall into disease, separation and disharmony. To reconnect with reality, with wholeness and truth we must acknowledge our gifts and respect that Spirit has offered us a unique opportunity to work with them.

We all have psychic powers and can develop them to enrich our personal lives and to help others either professionally or personally. However, these gifts operate best when the primary concern is for human needs, which means having a level of compassion for all living creatures. Psychic energy is at its most powerful when working with the power of love. Power is an energy to engage or express our personality in the world but love is the heart and truth of what channels through our gifts. When the desire for gain or prestige replaces the desire to learn and to serve, life will challenge these motivations and eventually things will go wrong.

Training

If you have discovered that you have psychic powers, it is important to get appropriate training. There are many good psychic colleges and organizations that teach psychic development. The training of psychics is usually undertaken by teachers who are themselves professional psychics and mediums. The apprentice learns by assisting a qualified and professional psychic and so integrates practical implementation of techniques into their own growing knowledge.

It is important to first learn about all the different types of psychic tools as if you are taking a foundation course. You would therefore learn about spirit communication, psychometry, auric readings, visualization, tuning into subtle energies and so on, in tandem with gradually awakening your gifts. Once you have a good grounding you can then specialize in a specific area, so some will lean towards mediumship and spirit communication, others to divination or healing. All the teachers of psychic development that I have spoken to regarding training recommend that the student takes at least a year to learn about the rules of psychic techniques, then begins to build their confidence on how to work with their talents in a safe and structured environment like a college or development group before working with people professionally.

There are enthusiastic psychics who wish to organize development circles and psychic groups without having adequate knowledge and experience. When you join a group, trust your instincts. Know yourself well enough to understand when you are unhappy about the group and do not feel safe. Most spirits are benevolent and only wish to communicate with the living for positive purposes but this is not always the case. This is why many successful mediums take a long time before they practise – it takes experience to understand the spirit world and to be adequately prepared and protected.

Your Spiritual Journey

Look over your life so far and map the course of your spiritual journey. Where has Spirit inspired you and touched your life? Your journey might include mystical experiences where you were touched by Spirit, visits to places of beauty and power that inspire you, encounters with ghosts or spirits that have touched you, psychic phenomena that has confirmed to you that there is another dimension. You may have read books, listened to music, met inspiring people, had insights and thoughts that have touched your soul. These events, influences or

experiences may not be specifically religious, or conventionally mystical; if a film or personal experience has changed your life, then include it. Review your journey: what patterns, significant factors and connections do you see? Which features are continually repeated? These insights enable you to discover how your spiritual journey has encouraged the development of your natural psychic powers and vice-versa.

Awakening the Professional

To begin your professional life as a psychic you will need a purpose. What do you want to do with your psychic talents in your life now? Do you want to become a professional medium? Or read tarot cards? Or learn how to use your psychic powers to interpret information at work? Or just to get on in business? If you work in a caring service, such as the medical profession or social services, do you want to use your intuitive skills to help you do a better job?

Once you have recognized the opportunities in your life to work with your psychic powers, then the true recognition of this gift will begin to evolve. I have found over the many years that I have been working, that many gifted psychics use their talents only privately with friends and family, rather than on public platforms, while others are better suited to a more public life and work with people on stage, privately and in workshops. Once you have made a decision that you will work with your psychic powers then the journey ahead embraces many challenges.

Ali Woozley – a practising midwife

'I grew up in the outback in Western Australia, where I formed a close relationship with the Australian earth and discovered the Aboriginal spirit guide who has guided and supported me through many challenges and difficulties in my life. Even at an early age I understood the cycles of birth and death and have never had a fear of death. My family moved to England where I continued to have a very free childhood with lots of psychic experiences. Gradually, I became aware of my natural psychic connection. I found that I could see people's auras, and discovered a natural healing talent. I also began to see people's spirit guides and even past lives. Whilst in meditation in an ashram in upstate New York, I had a vision that I had to become a midwife. I fulfilled that vision in 1992. My aim is to provide good care to women and families within a holistic framework.

This is how I integrate my psychic powers into my work:

- The night before I go on duty I avoid alcohol.
- I pay attention to any dreams that I have before work.
- I 'feed' myself with positive energy from books, attitudes and affirmations.
- I try to take time out for myself, i.e. through yoga, acupuncture, massage, swimming, walking in nature …
- It's obvious but I always make sure I am physically clean before going to work – it's like washing my home self away and bringing in my work self.
- I also shower after a tiring shift before leaving work, so I don't take the energy home.
- Before entering the hospital I always say a prayer such as, 'Dear God, and all the good women spirits protect me and the women in my care today.'
- I use essential oils, either in a burner or in massage oil.
- Humour is very important and can serve as a psychic protection tool – 'laugh it off' and you keep things in perspective.
- I research any issues or situations I have come across in my work, always learning.
- When working with a birthing mother, I try to keep myself protected as I need to separate myself to see what is really going on in the process of labour. First I remind myself that this is their experience not mine. I breathe deeply, I encourage the woman to breathe and anyone else in the room, as the breath is the midwives' best friend! I make sure my feet are firmly on the ground and imagine long roots going down into the earth. This helps me centre my energy and focus.
- In the second stage of labour, I often squat down. When I feel my pelvis opening I feel it keeps me open to encourage the woman to be open as well. I send a prayer out to the earth mother to take over the situation. I empathize with the woman and pay attention to what is happening in my body as I reflect what process the woman is going through. If I get an ache or a tug in an area I check it and usually find that it needs my attention.
- When the baby is birthed, I always welcome the baby and I say a prayer to the soul of the child and welcome him or her into the earth, immediately afterwards I stand back to give the family space to welcome the baby.
- Sometimes I get flashes of images, people or situations which seem out of context. These are often accompanied with a little bright blue flashing light, like a floating pin prick. I ask the woman if this means anything to them, as it might be their relative or ancestor who's come to be with them and to protect the child who has been born. I sense if it is a man or woman and if it is related to the mother or father. In most cases I have found that my instinct is right.
- At the end of each shift I thank God in a prayer for the experience and the chance to learn and grow.

As time goes on and I gather more experience in my work, I realize the responsibility of passing on knowledge to others. Getting involved in teaching junior staff and supporting the team gives positive feedback. In any "caring" job it is easy to take on the client's psychic baggage having a good caring relationship with other staff helps us to debrief and protect each other and ourselves.'

Craig Hamilton Parker – medium and author

'I am currently training people in chat rooms on the Internet. The first thing that I teach is the code of conduct, then mediumship and the law. As well as teaching people to practise clairvoyance, I work as a medium and communicate with Spirit. I connect with a spirit person in a form of telepathy, I "see", "hear" and "feel" the spirit using the gifts of clairvoyance, clairaudience and clairsentience.

As a child I could see lights around people's heads. This is what I now know to be the human aura, which people with clairvoyant sight can see. As a child I was more aware than most of people's moods – even when they were away from me. I could read people's thoughts from an early age and during my teens I began to see spirits.

I didn't always want to be a medium despite having the gift from an early age. I also had a sceptical side and part of me rejected the idea of working with my psychic powers. I travelled, worked as a painter and then a graphic designer, before the break up of my first marriage led me to bring up a baby by myself. I was determined to keep working, so I took the opportunity to demonstrate mediumship at the local spiritualist church every Sunday evening. I found it a little "churchy" and old fashioned but it was a good way to train up my skills as a medium. At the time of the break up of my marriage I met the medium Doris Stokes, who urged me to develop my gift and told me that I would one day do the same as she does. At the time this was a preposterous idea – I had a baby and a business to run. Soon after meeting Doris I met another medium Peter Close, who insisted that I join his new psychic development circle. His spirit guide told him that I was the one who was to complete the circle. Eventually I met my current wife, Jane, and being a medium, a teacher and author became my whole life.

The Internet has become a major part of my work nowadays. The beauty of working through the Internet is that there are no signals from clients, such as facial expressions or body language, to distract your psychic connection so you have an open forum to truly use your gift. I give readings to people over the Internet by email, using the I Ching as an oracle. If you want to develop your psychic powers and work on the Internet, you must trust what comes from inside you not just what the oracle says, as each person you are working with is a unique individual. Oracles can be a useful mirror of intuition but at the end of the day it is down to you to use your own psychic power to tune into each person that you work with. By not being able to be drawn into the physical response of each client, you are working in a pure connected way with no expectations or judgment. I always recommend to my students that they spend time practising with a few different methods of giving readings to find out which suits their personality best.

Also remember that everyone is different, sometimes you will be great at giving a reading, other times not so good. This is not always due to your ability, but the conditions may not be quite right, or the client is not feeling well or it is the wrong time. It is important when working as a psychic that you believe in yourself but also in the spirit of modesty.

This is my advice on working as a psychic.

- Always work with a code of conduct and make sure you know about the Fraudulent Mediums Act. In essence it warns you that you are not allowed to predict the future, only to make suggestions, i.e., "My advice is …, And to gain these types of results you could do …", etc. Always remind people that we all have the free will to change the course of destiny.
- Work with your common sense: never predict someone's death, always leave clients feeling uplifted and ready to deal with their problems, rather than see a fatalistic outcome.
- When a new client comes to see you for a reading always spend a few moments getting them relaxed – chat casually with them without fishing for information. Explain what you do and suggest that they can ask you any questions rather than trying to read between the lines.
- Never work with paraphernalia – get rid of headscarves, incense, etc., and keep the session as ordinary as possible. We want people to see psychics as normal people with a special gift. You don't need to impress people if you truly have the gift.
- If your client wishes to tape the session, ask if what you see in the reading will disturb their partner or family members. If so, suggest they don't tape it or ensure that they keep the tape safe. Be cautious, particularly about other parties.'

Helen Fost – practising psychotherapist and astrologer

'Astrology as a tool for psychic awareness is different from any of the other tools available in that it provides a totally new frame of reference, a rich and complex symbolic language with

which to observe and to describe the world. Symbols are connected with the power of the unconscious, with imagination, intuition and the collective or "transpersonal" level. This is the level at which psychic awareness happens. Working with symbols is one of the most powerful ways of opening up the mind to the intuitive intelligence that lies beyond its continual habit of verbalization.

Normally, we observe life out of our own personal experience and we classify it according to past experience or passed-on experience from others. We may observe patterns, coincidences, but it is hard to put together a coherent, objective perspective of what is going on. This is because the mind tends to focus on the manifest world, the point where things happen, where processes come to the surface. And so we miss seeing a world of connections, a world of potential. Astrology is about the world of potential, about seeing connections which are invisible to the everyday mind, catching the significance of what lies behind a certain incident, a relationship dynamic, a coincidence. Intuition or psychic awareness is the capacity to perceive this level of unmanifest reality, and it does not require astrology to do that. But astrology provides a language which acts like a new perceptual filter, offering a wide angle lens or a close up view, showing the relationship of the tiniest detail to the bigger picture, thus revealing unsuspected connections and giving definition and meaning to what lies behind the world of appearances.

HOW DOES THIS WORK?

The birth chart is a kind of mandala, a flat circular image of the sky, showing the position of the planets in the zodiacal signs at the moment of birth. In fact a chart does not belong to a person, it belongs to a moment, and it describes the very specific, complex and rich "energy field" of that moment in space and time. Astrologers observe this energy field in relation to the continually moving cycles of the planets, the ticking of the cosmic clock. And according to the positions and interrelations of the planets in the zodiac they can "see" the atmosphere with its inherent paradox, the richness and challenges of apparent contradictions. In combination with an intuitive tuning in to a person they can then unfold the background of what may be already manifesting in the person's life, as well as the untapped or emerging potential.

ASTROLOGY AS A TOOL FOR PREDICTION

Because the planets in the sky keep moving through the zodiac they are continually making new relationships or aspects to their original positions in the birthchart. This is what stimulates our inner and outer experiences, whether they appear to "happen" to us or we choose to make them happen. These movements are what challenge us to grow and change and discover more of our true potential. It is not that the planets make things happen in our lives but rather that they are themselves dancing to a cosmic music which we are all part of but cannot directly perceive. So their dance can inform us, through their symbolic meaning, about the energetic influences we are experiencing.

Exploring the complex symbolism of the chart it is possible to get an objective and detailed view of what is going on: when the process started, or is going to start, when it will finish, what other background issues are involved, how the changes are likely to manifest and above all, what is the purpose of it all. This does not involve judgments about good and bad, it is rather like putting together a jigsaw puzzle to reveal the wisdom and the healing that is carried by the wholeness of the picture.

Astrology shows us that what is happening for us "out there" in the world is a reflection of something going on "in here" in us. Thus it enables us to shift our perspective onto the over-all context of what is happening rather than dealing only with the content of what is happening, which leads to a totally different outlook on how we experience our lives and how we make choices for the future.'

Angela Watkins – facilitator, medium and teacher at the college of psychic studies

'The gift I have is to be able to give evidence of life after death. Normally when I work the spirit people come and give three or four pieces of evidence to their living family to prove that it is them. When I am working on stage, I can usually sense who I need to talk to – it is as if I cannot take my eyes off the person. I can hear and see Spirit, and they overshadow my energy. I have three guides who work with me: one is a gentle Indian woman who deals with family matters, another is a Tibetan monk who gives me his wisdom, and the third is a warrior spirit who directs and closes down the energy after spirit communication.

My most powerful evidential experience happened at a Spiritualist church in London. As I was preparing to give a demonstration of mediumship, I became aware of the spirit of a young woman. I asked if she would mind coming back later when I had begun but she said "I want you to give my mother a message … I have got the same name as your dog, Holly". She told me which pew her mother was sitting in and that she was very beautiful, she then told me that she would come back later. After giving evidence to an elderly lady, I counted the pews and there was the mother. The spirit of the girl came and she began by describing her funeral – even the tin trays filled with sand where they placed lit candles. She mentioned the family cat and a necklace her mother had given her. The mother denied knowing anything about a

necklace until the spirit of the girl said that she would wind it round her wrist as a bracelet. The mother then realized that it really was her daughter. She had been going to the church twice a week for 18 months waiting for a message from her daughter and was overjoyed that her daughter was safe. Many spirits will wait months even years until they find a medium that they would have liked if they were alive – spirits, like us, seek compatibility.

This is my advice to up-and-coming mediums and psychics.

- Recognize your gift, let it unfold naturally and receive professional training.
- Realize that you cannot heal and help everyone.
- Always know that you can ask Spirit for what assistance you need.
- Look after your health and well-being and never work if you are feeling out of balance or ungrounded.
- Before you begin to work in a session or on a platform always ask your spirit guides and your god to clear the space and to protect your energy when you work. Before I begin to work I prepare the room by opening the windows, clearing the energy by ringing bells and using candlelight, incense or smudging with sage. I ask for protection and then prepare myself mentally for the session and call in the doorkeeper guide to ensure full protection from the spirit world.
- Always close down after working. If I am working on the platform, I always leave before the audience and do not mix with them. I close down privately, as some people will draw your energy as they will still be seeking support and help.
- When I give private sittings I always make sure that I make the client feel relaxed and explain what I am going to do and how it works. When working from home I always ask them if they have had a sitting before. If they haven't I explain to them that it's a bit like having a chat. I look quite normal when communicating with Spirit, I receive information and give the messages. If I mention Spirit I clarify that they are not walking around the room. It is important that the client is relaxed and feels safe. I ask them to come with a smile and an open mind.
- I ask my guides to help with the sitting and ensure that I close down after the person leaves.

Truly gifted psychics are always chosen for their role by the spirits of the universe, for working in a spiritual capacity is not a self-elected vocation. Someone who determines to become a psychic as an ego-enhancing and money-making exercise will not truly succeed. Psychic gifts run in the family. When a person is called to work with their gifts they may attempt to avoid the calling and for very good reasons – psychic work is one of the most demanding of vocations and it is a 24-hour a day job that requires them to be available simultaneously to the spirit world and to their clientele.

Thankfully, people today are becoming more liberated in their views and recognize that modern spirituality addresses contemporary problems and helps people reconnect with their soul and find solutions to everyday physical, emotional and spiritual issues.'

A Final Word

The practices in this book can be very powerful, please do not attempt any of them if you are suffering from any mental instability, or taking consciousness-changing drugs or potent medications.

The use of these practices outside a strong personal ethical framework is inappropriate and sometimes dangerous. All writers and teachers have a responsibility to their readers and students to guide them safely to effective skills and methods that can be reproduced. In any book where the writer cannot personally supervise the reader's training, there is always the danger that the reader's interest in dynamic techniques may outrun an ethical and moral foundation. Psychic training is usually undertaken in the context of sound and supportive development groups and colleges. Be aware that this work has a real effect, do nothing if your intentions are vague or unfocused. If you find any of the techniques offered in this book too difficult, just stop doing them until you feel ready. Take responsibility for your experiences and always trust your instincts.

Resources

I have recommended a number of educational centres and colleges who specialize in psychic or spiritual development, including a small selection of practitioners, magazines and publications. You should contact services in your local area to find recommended places where you can study or find supplies to supplement your psychic powers.

Magazines and publications

LIGHT MAGAZINE
This magazine, published by the College of Psychic Studies, covers a wide spectrum of articles on psychic and spiritual subjects (for contact details, see address below).

PSYCHIC NEWS
Weekly newspaper covering the Spiritualist movement and the many psychics and mediums who work in this field throughout the UK. Available from:
Psychic News
The Coach House
Stansted Hall
Stansted
Essex CM24 8UI
UK
E-mail: pn@snu.org.uk

KINDRED SPIRIT
The leading guide to mind/body/spirit subjects in the UK, this quarterly journal includes features and articles, a comprehensive resource directory of contacts and a mail order section. Available from:
Kindred Spirit
Foxhole
Dartington
Totnes
Devon TQ9 6EB
UK
Tel: +44 (0) 1803 866686
Fax: +44 (0) 1803 866591
E-mail: editors@kindredspirit.co.uk
Website: www.kindredspirit.co.uk

PSYCHIC TYMES
A bimonthly paranormal ezine on the Web.
Website: www.psychic-tymes.com

Meditation Centres

THE KRISHNAMURTI CENTRE
A place to restore the spirit and learn about meditation and the teachings of J. Krishnamurti, a noted Indian teacher.
The Krishnamurti Centre
Brockwood Park
Bramdean
Hants SO24 OLQ
UK
Tel: +44 (0) 1962 771748
Fax: +44 (0) 1962 771875
Website: www.kfoundation.org

YOGANANDA CENTRE
Meditation centre based on the spiritual teachings of yogananda.
Website: www.yogananda-srf.org

SIVANANDA ASHRAM YOGA FARM
Offers four-week intensive teacher training courses.
14651 Ballantree Lane
Grass Valley
California
95949 USA
Tel: (800) 469 9642
Fax: (530) 477 6054
E-mail: yogafarm@sivananda.org
Website: www.sivananda.org/farm

TIBETAN MEDITATION RETREAT
Kagyu Samye Ling Tibetan Centre
Eskdalemuir
Langholm
Dumfrieshire
Scotland DG13 0QL
Tel: + 44 (0) 1387 373232
Runs retreats and workshops based on Tibetan
Buddhism.

FINDHORN FOUNDATION
The Park
Forres
Scotland IV36 0TS
Tel: + 44 (0) 1309 691653
Fax: + 44 (0) 1309 691663
Runs workshops and retreats about Nature spirits,
ecological consciousness, meditation and spirituality.

SACRED HEALER RETREATS
Email: natalia@sacredhealers.co.uk
Weekend retreats based on Celtic Shamanism in the
heart of the West Country, UK, facilitated by Natalia
and Terry O'Sullivan.
Information on www.soulrescuers.com on Celtic
Rituals and retreats.

Psychic Colleges and Organisations

COLLEGE OF PSYCHIC STUDIES
16 Queensberry Place
London SW7 2EB
Tel: + 44 (0) 20 7589 3292
E-mail: cpstudies@aol.com
Website: www.psychic-studies.org.uk
One of the best facilitated psychic colleges in
London, their programme covers a wide spectrum
of subjects including mediumship training, auras,
psychometry, psychic development and healing.

ALTERNATIVES
St James's Church
197 Piccadilly
London W1V OLL
Tel: + 44 (0) 20 7287 6711
Website: www.alternatives.org.uk
With 20 years experience in the mind, body and spirit
field, they offer a fantastic programme of lectures
and workshops from all leading UK, European and
American spiritual psychics and healers.

THE SCHOOL OF INSIGHT AND INTUITION
Tel: + 44 (0) 20 8979 0940
Email: insight.intuition@btinternet.com
Website: www.insightandintuition.com
Offers practical and comprehensive psycho-spiritual
development programmes both for personal awareness
and to become a professional practitioner in the
psychic and healing fields.

Spiritualism

SPIRITUALIST ASSOCIATION OF GREAT BRITAIN
33 Belgrave Square
London SW1 8QB
Tel: + 44 (0) 20 7235 3351
Offers daily public demonstrations of mediumship
with private sittings and workshops available with
qualified mediums.

THE WHITE EAGLE LODGE
New Lands
Brewells Lane
Rake
Liss
Hampshire QU33 7HY
Tel: + 44 (0) 1730 893300
Fax: + 44 (0) 1730 892235
E-mail: enquiries@whiteagle.org
A worldwide organization based on the mediumship
of Grace Cooke and the teachings of her guiding
spirit White Eagle.

THEOSOPHICAL SOCIETY
The Blavatsky Trust
Avalon
Little Weston
Sparkford
Yeovil BA22 7HP
Philosophical teachings of Madam Blavatsky, one
of the first European Mediums who channeled
discarnate spirits and gave teachings and spiritual
philosophy.

SOCIETY FOR PSYCHICAL RESEARCH
Worldwide Scientific Investigators Of Psychic
Phenomena
49 Marloes Road
London W8 6LA
Tel/Fax: + 44 (0) 20 7937 8984
Website: www.spr.ac.uk

Practitioners

TERRY O'SULLIVAN
E-mail: terry@sacredhealers.co.uk
Website: www.soulrescuers.com
For soul rescue, space clearing and shamanic healing. Terry is one of Britain's leading authorities on ghosts and hauntings.

DAVINA MACKAIL
Tel: + 44 (0) 20 8789 4545
E-mail: Davina@mackail.co.uk
Website: www.mackail.co.uk
For space clearing, shamanic healing and psychic counselling.

KAREN BECKER
lamemedicinewoman@aol.com
Tel: (818) 543-1739.
Native American Clairvoyant, bodyworker and healer.

DR ANGELA WATKINS Ph.d, S.R.N, O.N.C.
Tel: + 44 (0) 20 7589 3292
Medium and clairvoyant. Contact the College of Psychic Studies in London to join her courses on psychic development, spirit communication and mediumship. She is available for private sittings at the college.

HELEN FOST B.A. Hons. (Oxon) M.A. D.F. Astrol.
Astrologer, psychotherapist and hypnotherapist. She has a diploma from the Faculty of Astrological Studies and has been working with astrology for over 12 years. She also has training in Biodynamic Psychotherapy, NLP, Process Oriented Psychology, Time Therapy and hypnosis. She is currently training as an inter-faith minister. She sees clients in London, Oxford and Rome and also does phone sessions with clients worldwide.

Tel: + 44 (0) 1491 612233
E-mail: hfrost@astrotherapy.info
Website: www.astrotherapy.info

CRAIG HAMILITON PARKER
Medium and clairvoyant. Available for readings on the web and join his teaching programmes via the website: www.psychics.co.uk

Dowsing

BRITISH SOCIETY OF DOWSERS
Sycamore Barn
Tamley Lane
Hastingleigh
Ashford
Kent TN25 5HW
UK
Tel: +44 (0) 1233 750253
Email: secretary@britishdowsers.org
Website: www.britishdowsers.org

ASSOCIATION OF SCOTTISH DOWSERS
Riccarton Mill
Newcastleton
Roxburghshire TD9 0SQ
Scotland

AMERICAN SOCIETY OF DOWSERS INC.
Danville
Vermont 05828-0024
Tel: (802) 684 3417
Fax: (802) 684 2565

Acknowledgements

Thank you to my project editor Kate Latham for her tireless support and to all the staff at Thorsons. To all my wonderful contributors including Terry O'Sullivan, Sheenagh Shirley, Angela Watkins, Helen Fost, Davina Mackail, Craig Hamilton Parker, Ali Woozley, Taryn Hill, Theresa Beaumont, Suzanna McInerney, and a big thank you to my closest friends and allies and unpaid editors Nicola Graydon and Elaine Pierson.

Index